D1251130

Harriet Quick

Catwalking

A History of the fashion model

THE WELLFLEET PRESS
WELLFLEET

Publishing Director: Laura Bamford
Executive Editor: Mike Evans
Editor: Humaira Husain
Production: Melanie Frantz
Picture Research: Wendy Gay
Art Director: Keith Martin
Executive Art Editor: Mark Winwood
Design: Birgit Eggers

Special thanks to British Vogue for their time, effort and contribution
from their unique archive.
The name NOVA © IPC Magazine Ltd

This edition first published by Wellfleet Press, a division of Book Sales Inc,
114 Northfield Avenue, Edison, New Jersey 08837

First published in 1997 by Hamlyn, an imprint of Octopus Publishing Group Limited,
2-4 Heron Quays, London E14 4JB

Copyright © 1997 Octopus Publishing Group Limited

ISBN 0-7858-1093-5

Produced by Toppan
Printed and bound in Hong Kong

walking Cat

History of the fashio

del

Cat
walking
A History of
n model

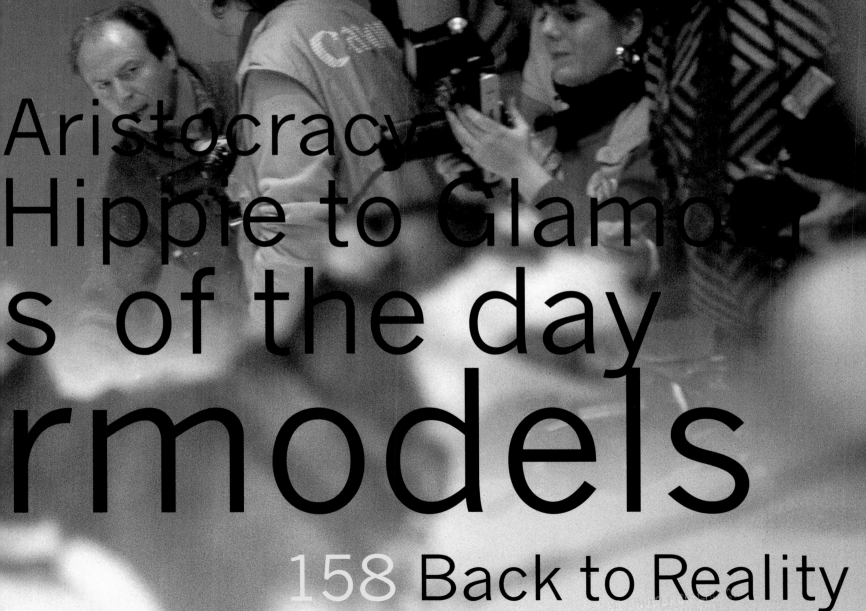

Aristocracy
Hippie to Glamo
s of the day
rmodels
158 Back to Reality

'The living mannequin is a woman who must be more feminine than all other women.'

'Make no mistake about it being glamorous. Every day is hardwork and modelling far from being a world of fantasy is one of harsh facts.'

'I'm only interested in the external features – How can I photograph the soul?'

'You feel like a clotheshorse having its outside layer ripped off with a paint stripper and then reapplied several times a day.'

oder fierungen eine vngeferlich zweyer finger breyt/ Darn
also gemacht / das man es höher oder niderer richten mag
hinaus in zimlicher weitten dz corpus so du conterfeten wilt/
weg hindersich vnd hab dein aug zu dem absehen.o. negst d
vñ ob es recht nach deinem willen lig/ Darnach stell dz git
absehen also/ wilt du wenig lucken oder fierungen begreiffen
besich wie vil dz corpus im gitter lucken begreuf nach leng v
auf ein bappir oder tafel darein du conterfeten wilt/ vnd si
das Corpus/ vnd was du in yder fierung des gitters findest
hast das ist gut vnd gerecht/ Wilt du aber für das spitzig a
eben so gut/ solcher meynung hab jch hernach ein form auf

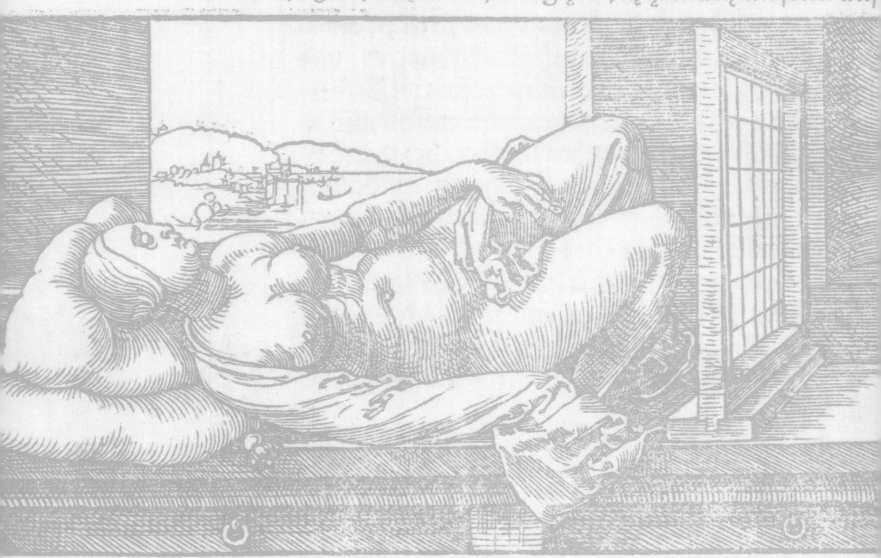

Inspiring Beauties

Before popular fashion evolved in the early twentieth century, icons of beauty and fashion were set by the ruling classes and immortalized by artists and sculptors. The only type of model in the public's conscious, was the artist's model. Through the centuries the model has experienced numerous transformations. She has been cast as Madonna, Magadelena, Nymph, hero, slave, humble peasant and fecund Venus. At the turn of the century, the artist's model became a subject of art itself in Manet's watershed work *Dejeuner Sur L'Herbe* of 1853. The artist's model is pictured nude and triumphant at the centre of the canvas. *Dejeuner Sur L'Herbe* caused an outcry amongst polite Parisian society. **Manet** not only had made the model the subject of the work, he made her a subject of envy. For centuries, the artist's model had been stereotyped as female nude, with a reputation little better than that of a whore. Victorine Meurent, Manet's red haired milky skinned muse was the first model to be seen as an individual.

In the twentieth century, as abstract art triumphed, the artist's model literally fell out of the picture. The camera offered an accuracy of representation which the artist could never hope to achieve, so where questions of beauty and fashion were concerned, the fashion photographer and the fashion model in the popular media of the magazine set the standards. Over the course of the 20th century, the model image has come to represent the changing ideal of woman.

The artist's model is the fashion model's natural antecedent. Both pose for a living and both share a similar history. The artist's model started off a nameless body and ended up the centre of the picture, over the twentieth century the fashion model has been raised from faceless clotheshorse and figure of opprobrium to become an international celebrity. Through time, in the model's history generation after generation has been coloured by scandal and prejudice.

As far back as the 15th century, the art critic and diarist **Vasari**, the equivalent of Nigel Dempster to Renaissance Italy, reported on model gossip. In *Lives of The Artists* he opinions that the only model stories worth recounting are those involving aristocratic models in scandalous relationships. Of the modern celebrity fashion model , newspaper editors today share the same judgement. By the 1800s, society had become so intrigued by the model's profession, she generated her own form of popular fiction. Daphne du Maurier's *Trilby* was one of a spate of books which told a tale of the wayward model involved in a passionate relationship with the genius male artist. *Trilby* was a period best seller. A century later, the fashion model was to become the subject of film and fiction. The 1966 film *Blow Up* starring the model Veruschka as a nymphomaniac beauty and David Hemmings as a sex mad photographer, has a similar plot. Beauty, erotica and scandal: the model has a rich history.

Accounts of the first models originate from Ancient Greece of 400 B.C. It is because man wanted to idealise his own kind, that the job of the model was born. Quite simply, artists and sculptors needed base material from which to work. Pliny the Elder in *The Natural History* recounts the story of the young artist **Xeuxis** on his search for models amongst the people of Crotona. Offered all the young women in the town, Xeuxis could find no one figure who fulfilled his ideal. As a solution, the artist chose five female models the sum of whose physical attributes he considered perfection. Xeuxis literally collaged their body parts together to create an ideal. A similar paste technique has become common practice in fashion photography. With the aid of sophisticated printing methods and computer technology, technicians can airbrush or superimpose body parts – hands, feet, legs, breasts – to create perfect model images out of less than perfect bodies.

In the fourth century B.C. models were valued for their body parts rather than beauty. According to Frances Borzello in *Notes From the Artist's Model* artists gathered men and women from the streets: a cripple with an overdeveloped chest could be the subject of study, likewise a woman who simply bore a beautiful neck and shoulders. The raw material was often rough, but the ideals which the artists realised have remained unsurpassed. Statues have been studied and copied by artists for centuries. Live models were even trained to ape their poses in the late 18th century. The Royal Academy went as far as to install elaborate pulley systems to enable the models to hold their heroic Greek poses. The Greek ideal influenced fashion photography in the 20th century. Before the profession of the fashion model was established with its repertoire of poses, the fashion photographer Hoyningen-Huene and his pupil Horst who worked for *Vogue* in the Thirties, learnt the art of form and gesture by studying the statues housed in The Louvre.

The Greek ideal was cast away as Christianity swept through Western civilizations. During the Middle Ages, the purpose of art was to inspire devotion. Artists copied figure illustrations rather than work from the live model. To take inspiration from a human figure would have been considered sinful.

The picture changed during the Italian Renaissance. As society tried to understand the mysteries of life, artists tried to uncover its mysteries in art. The human form became a serious subject of study. Models were measured, weighed, drawn and redrawn as artists attempted to develop a theory of beauty. The inquiry was deeply serious. Artists went as far as to dissect bodies in order to understand the inner workings of the body. Alberti, an acclaimed art theorist wrote in his book *On Painting*: 'Before dressing a man we first draw him nude, then we enfold him in draperies so in painting the nude we place first his bones and muscles which we then cover with flesh so that it is not difficult to understand where each muscle is beneath.'

Torso of Aphrodite: a Roman copy of the Greek original by Praxiteles, 350 BC

Leonardo da Vinci (1452-1519) drawing of head and eye

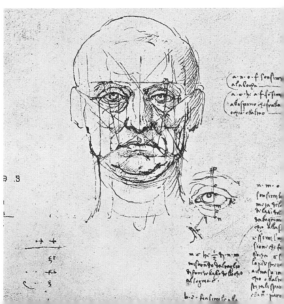

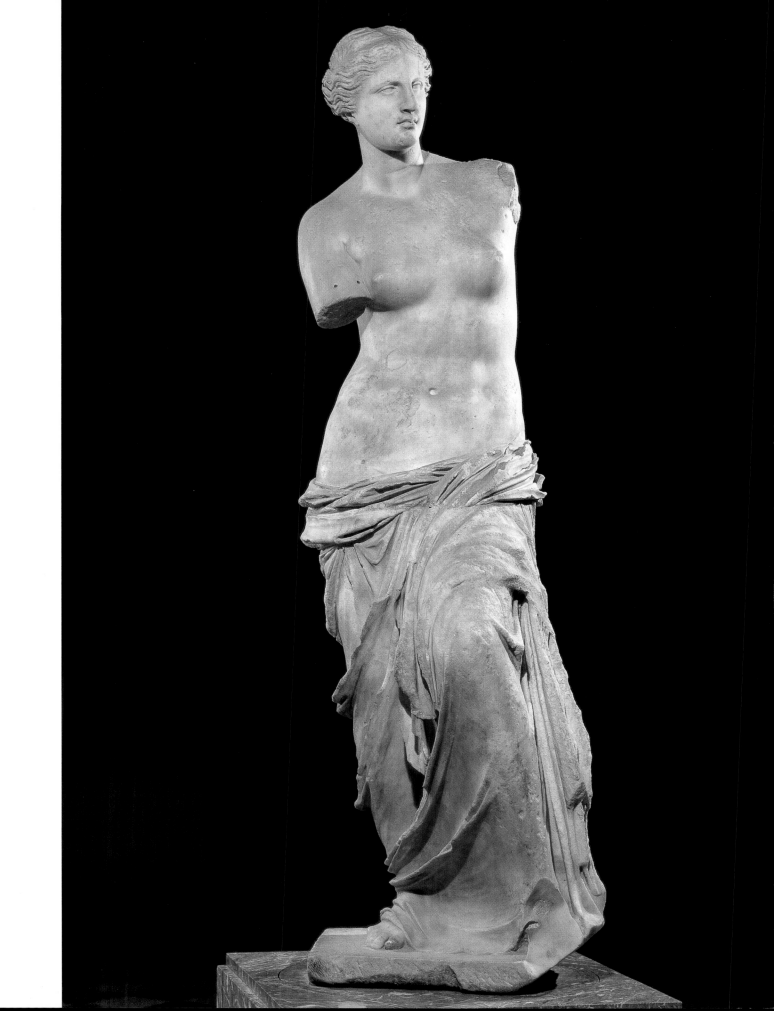

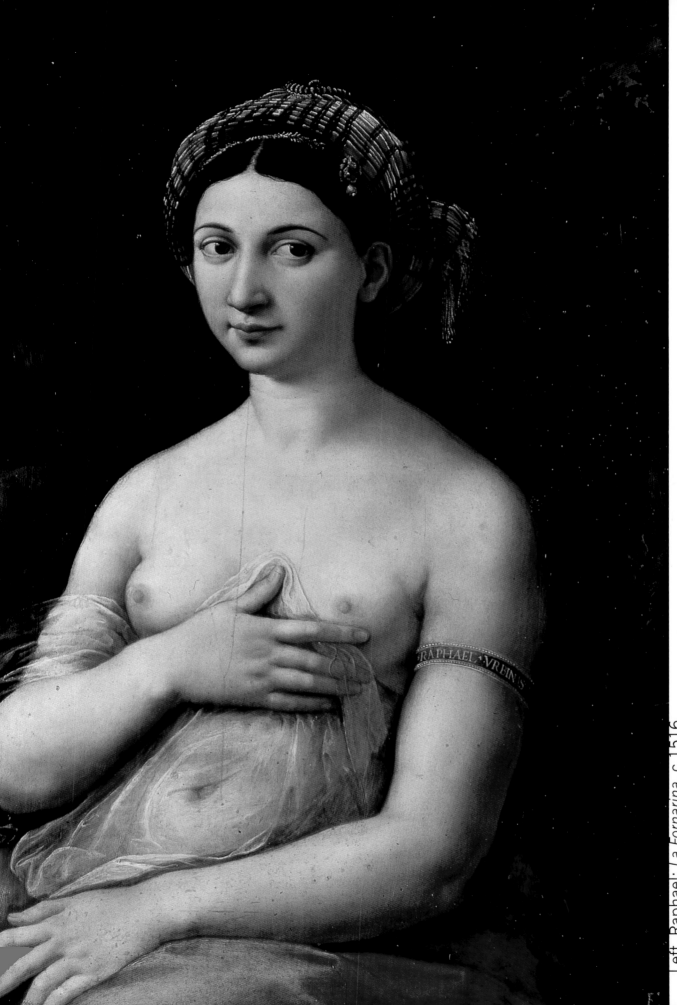

Left, Raphael: *La Fornarina*, c.1516
Far Left, Raphael: *Galatea*, 1513 from a fresco at Villa Farnesina, Rome

It was during The Renaissance that the female model first developed her scandalous public image. Tabloid writers of the day found rich pickings in behind the scenes gossip. Vasari in *Lives of the Artists* tells the story of the fresco painter **Fra Lippo Lippi** who abandons his beloved metier to elope with **Lucrezia**, his beautiful model. The story is dramatic. Lucrezia makes a dangerous escape from the local convent to join her beloved. Vasari also wrote of **Raphael's** passionate romance with **La Fornarina,** his model and muse. The affair has been recounted many times, even finding its expression in art. Through to the 20th century, the true nature of the affair remained heavily coded: 'He loved her body, he loved her grossly...but he imposed silence upon his desires, the lover in him did not suppress the artist. They developed a code of morals different from those of other mortals, they developed a sense and liking for variety,' writes art critic Angelo Rappoport. (*Artists and Their Models* 1910).

Picasso got down to the nitty gritty thirty years later. In an engraving, Raphael is pictured mid coitus with La Fornarina amongst the palettes and draperies of his studio. The onlooker is the artist, Picasso himself.

The public has maintained an insatiable appetite for the model story. In art the model/artist relationship became a genre. According to Borzello, the German artist **Dürer**, a contemporary of Vasari, was the first to establish the stereotype visually. In a pen and ink drawing of 1532, Dürer shows the artist peering through a filigree screen (a metaphor for the canvas), the other side of which lies a model who is seen legs apart and skirts up to her chin. In the 20th century, the behind-the-scenes affairs of fashion have proved equally scandalous. The big affairs began with Lee Miller and Man Ray in the 1920s, and reached a peak of scandal with David Bailey and Jean Shrimpton. By the 1970s the model/photographer affair was considered standard practice.

Left, Jan Vermeer: Artist in his Studio, 1665/6

Below, Peter Paul Rubens, Head of a Child

A further revolution in the model's history came with the Dutch artists of the seventeenth century. Artists, relieved from the pressures of court and state patronage, were able to develop a secular art. For the first time real life, real people became the subject of art. As in previous centuries, models were found amongst family and friends but they were painted as themselves. The stiff classical body shapes made way for natural gestures, flawless skin supplanted by ruddy pimpled complexions; there was no single uniform ideal. Artists pursued their own aesthetics.
Rubens adored plump, fleshy women, his wives Isabella Brandt and Helen Fourment were his most celebrated subjects. **Rembrandt** painted more soulful characters. His mother posed for the artist's old and humble women, his wife, the auburn haired Saskia van Ulemburgh, is clearly recognisable in several works including the *Young Jewish Girl.* The fascination with reality versus art led **Vermeer** to take the subject as an inquiry in itself.

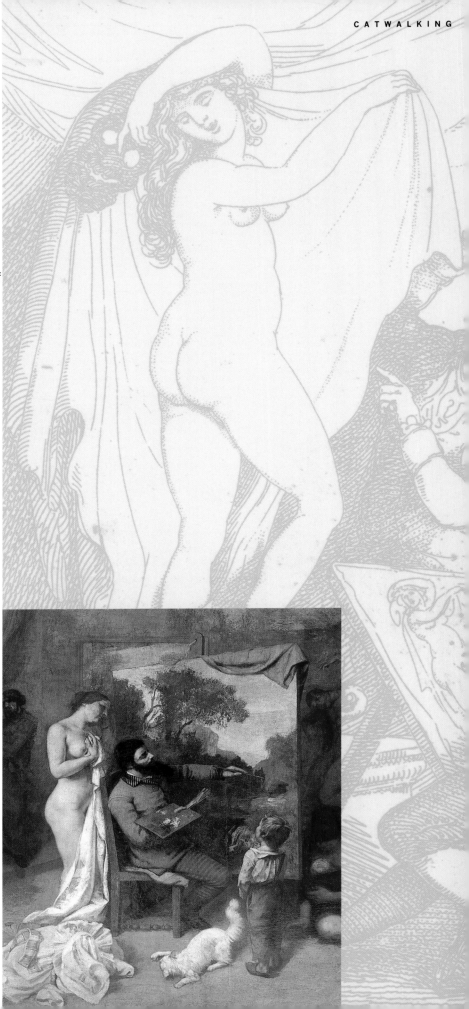

Whereas realism dominated art in the 17th century, artifice triumphed in the 18th. Modelling for artists became the rage, as the aristocratic patrons of art delighted in the art of make believe. The aristocracy and the marquise alike offered their services to the male artist and delighted in their pictorial transformations. Boucher, Watteau, artists employed by the court, were able to play off the jealous rivals of the *haute* and *demi monde*, assigning a hierarchy of characters to their various subjects. Famous courtesans **Madame du Pompadour** and **Madame du Barry** were made as beautiful and fashionable as the blue blooded royals. And as their popularity increased, so did the number of canvasses they appeared in. Model spotting became a new political sport.

The 18th century witnessed another important turnaround in the model's history – professional status. Establishment of the first schools of art such as London's Royal Academy (1752) made way for the change. Life drawing was considered an essential part of the artist's training, and it was by virtue of the Academy system that models were able to find regular employment and regular pay. The Royal Academy paid 4 shillings an hour plus beer money to male models while female models, harder to find, were paid twice as much. Female modelling was considered taboo. The stigma was so great that the Academy, desperate to preserve its reputation, stipulated that no outsiders, bar the Royal Family, could enter a female life class. The Academy system effectively gave credence and kudos to both the artist and the model. Modelling started to attract respectable types, even aristocratic women who were attracted by a new breed of gentleman artist, offered their services.

Once again modelling became a hotbed of scandal and the story of the aristocratic model and male artist, which Vasari had made his forte during the Renaissance, was revived. **Thomas Rowlandson**, a student at The Academy and later a celebrated cartoonist and pornographic artist, lampooned the trend in a pen and ink work in which a rapturous Lady Hamilton posing as a Greek Goddess is surrounded by gentleman artists drooling at her feet.

Gustave Courbet: detail from The Studio

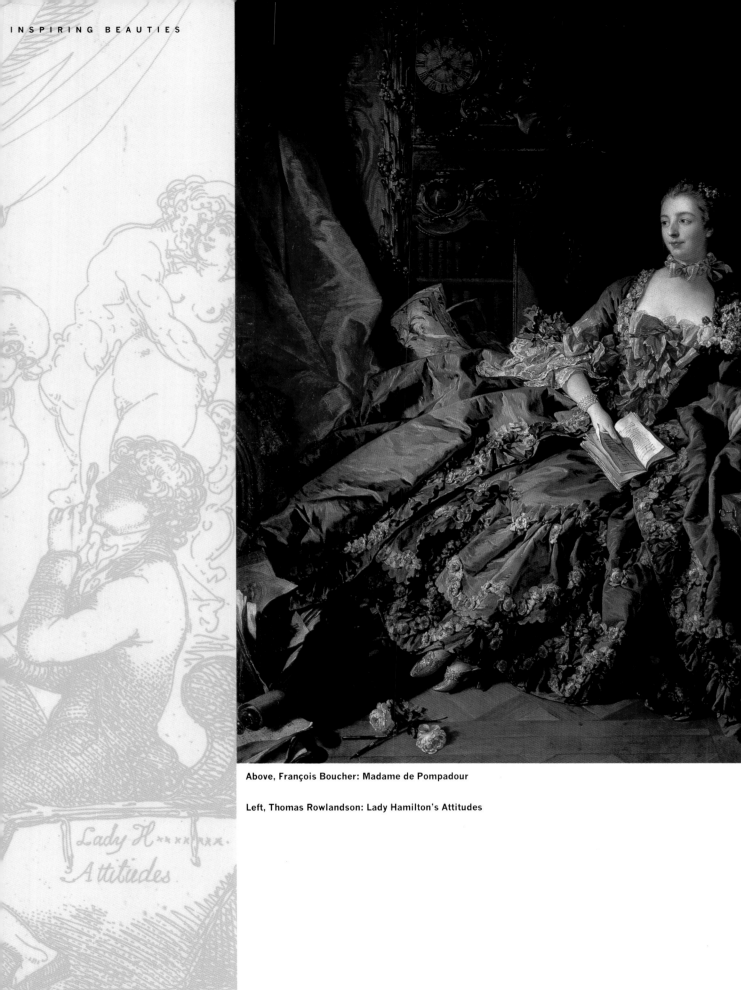

Above, François Boucher: Madame de Pompadour

Left, Thomas Rowlandson: Lady Hamilton's Attitudes

Sir John Everett Millais: *Ophelia* 1851/2

The profession of the model was established in the 18th century, and the romantic stereotype was allowed to blossom a century later. In the 19th century the female model came to be seen as an independent, adventure seeking woman and the artist, a genius. The new glamourous image of the model was propagated in Bohemia, the Parisian community which was set up mid-century by a group of radical artists. The community's principles, later to be inherited by the Hippie movement of the Sixties, were based on the ideals of free love and aesthetic and religious freedom. It was the artist's model, suggests Borzello, who became the symbol of Bohemia's ideals. The public was fascinated by Bohemia. Writers of the day fictionalised and glamourised the artistic lifestyle. Through journals and novels like **Daphne du Maurier's** *Trilby*, the model's public image experienced a radical change. No longer was the model considered whorish, she was seen as a pioneer, a beauty. In England, the 'star' models of the Pre-Raphaelite artists courted their own celebrity. **Elizabeth Siddal**, porcelain skinned and red headed, and **Jane Burden**, strong-featured and dark haired, set fashions in beauty. Women modelled themselves on Siddal and Burden, adopting their natural hair and flowing robes.

The exotic image was fuelled by the artists themselves. The Pre-Raphaelites blurred the division between reality and art; art became life, and life the substance of art; the artist idealised his model, and the model fell in love with the artist, Siddal married the drug-raddled painter **Rossetti**, Jane Burden, **William Morris**. Every aspect of life was romanticised, made artful; even the model hunt. In her biography **Diana Holman Hunt** descendant of one of these 'brotherhood artists' describes a model hunt: 'They roamed the streets with arms linked pursuing their prey – pretty girls were surrounded and captured like birds in a net.'

Dante Gabriel Rossetti: The Annunciation

The impressionist artists of the late nineteenth century can be credited for the model's final apotheosis. She became the subject of art itself. **Seurat** made his mission clear, he entitled a painting *Poseuses*, literally the models. It shows a group of young models undressing in the artist's studio. But the trump card must certainly go to **Edouard Manet's** *Dejeuner sur L'Herbe* in which Victorine Meurent, the artist's model and muse, takes part in an intellectual gathering, nude and triumphant.

The invention of photography made art's endeavour for reality appear futile. As art moved into the realm of abstracts, the model literally dropped out of the picture. In the public eye she was replaced by the fashion model. Over the following century, the fashion model's story echoed that of the artist's model. They both started life the opprobrium of society and turned into an equal. In the case of the fashion model the revolution took just ninety years.

Over the next century, the fashion model's story echoed that of the artist's model

Georges Seurat: Poseuses

Edouard Manet: Dejeuner Sur L'Herbe

The seeds of modelling

A Paquin design, 1920

Designers sent their best looking models to the races at Longchamp, Ascot and so on, to show off their designs amongst high society

The fashion model was born in the late 19th century, a

product of the industrial revolution. Her role did not exist before,
there were simply no clothes to sell. Fashion had been the preserve
of the aristocracy and marquise and its influence reached no further
than the palace walls. It was the emergence of the bourgeoisie in
the 19th century and the parallel development of the fashion
industry that paved the way for the model. Up until the late 19th
century, fashion had been prescribed by the client and made to
order by teams of dressmakers. Only when there were clothes and
designs to sell did the fashion model become a necessity.

An Englishman by the name of **Charles Frederick Worth**,

the first named couturier, 'invented' the fashion model. Worth
began his legendary career as a salesman in a fabric shop by the
name of Gagelin et Opigez in the Rue Richlieu, Paris. The shop
started to sell ready made garments, capes mantles and shawls –
and it was Worth's idea to show the clothes in motion to the clients.
He chose his models, or mannequins as they were known, from the
ranks of salesgirls and assistants. **Marie Vernet**, daughter of a
provincial tax officer, was one. Vernet was the first named fashion
model. She married Worth and moved with him to set up a dressmaking business in a small studio on the Left Bank in 1858. Worth
was a radical in his approach to design. Dressmaking had been a
purely service led business – the clients prescribed the outfits, the
dressmaker made them up – and the business was dominated by
women, until Worth male dressmakers were unheard of. It was
simply taboo to expose skin or to be touched by any man outside
wedlock. To overcome the sexual prejudice Worth 'employed' his
wife Vernet to model his designs.

To start, business was tough. Marie Vernet was sent

out in public to exhibit her husband's gowns. But gradually Worth's
reputation spread, and society's more outlandish women came to
be dressed by him. His brilliantly inventive designs eventually
attracted the attention of Princess Eugénie, the wife of the emperor
Napolean III, and notorious fun loving hostess of the Imperial Court.
Vernet herself was sent as an envoy to the Court, in order to present
her husband's ideas to the Princess. Worth followed, with a good
line in self promotion and diplomatic skills. Once the Imperial deal
was clinched, Worth's reputation was made.

Business thrived. In 1858, Worth employed twenty seam-stresses, by 1870 the count was 1200. Madame Worth remained his first and best advertisement. She attended race meetings and society events, she was the first to wear his walking skirt, crinoline free dress and daytime separates. Amongst polite society Vernet's face soon became known, and her fashion widely copied.

It is down to Worth's genius at self publicity that the first couture shows came into being. He developed the moving mannequins idea which he had first introduced at Gagelin et Opigez for his own business. At each season he invited his clients to view his latest designs in informal presentations at his studio. Initially the invitations were turned down; the notion of a client visiting a dressmaker with other clients was thought low class, but Worth was uncompromising, if women wanted to employ his skills, they had to come to him. The shows soon became a diary date on society's calendar. Madame Worth trained the models whom she selected from the workshop floor. They were neither tall or necessarily beautiful. As long as they showed the clothes, and walked in a straight line, that was enough. Worth's spectacles were a novelty in Paris society and attracted voyeurs as well as clients.

The novelist Goncourt writes in his journals, May 1876: 'A pretty detail of elegant Parisien life amongst the young models in the salons of Worth, who display and parade the robes of the illustrious couturier upon their svelte bodies, there is a girl, or rather a lady model, whose speciality is to represent pregnancy in high life. Seated all alone, in the half light of a boudoir, she exhibits before the eyes of lady visitors in an interesting condition, the toilette designed with the greatest genius for compensating for the ungainly appearance of being with child.'
At the couturier's death in 1895, Worth was a household fashion name. He established the fashion model, in his wife Marie Vernet, the fashion show and the foundations of the fashion business in the twentieth century.

Marie Vernet was the blueprint fashion model but she was accepted by society only as Worth's wife. The fashion model was to remain a figure of scorn and scandal for another twenty five years. It was to take the devastation of the First World War and the challenge of the Suffragette movement to shift perceptions, and radical work by the next generation of couturiers before the fashion model was finally recognised.

Anna Pavlova
The dancer Pavlova was featured on postcards, as were the images of many dancers and actresses at the turn of the century

Fashion was the pastime for the new moneyed leisure class. A show in 1910 at Wanamaker's department store, Philadelphia, from the Illustrated London News

1910

'Do not talk to the girls, they are not here,' Paul Poiret instructed the *Daily Mirror's* fashion editor Alison Settle during a 1920 show

Madame decides on her gowns at a Paris fashion show

In the early years of the 20th century, the fashion business grew apace. Women found new freedom, liberated on the one hand by education, and on the other by increased wealth. Sport and motoring became popular, but for a new breed of sophisticated woman nothing gave greater pleasure than fashion: 'The mode – the word alone was enough to send frissons down the spine of any ambitious young lady at the turn of the century. If one was not *au courant* with the mode one might as well stay in Hammond, Indiana, for the rest of your life, doomed to provincialism like Madame Bovary. The importance of the right clothes to aspiring womanhood in those years cannot be overestimated. A woman could fall on the quality of her gowns,' writes Edith Wharton in *The House of Mirth*.

A second generation of couturiers: **Paquin**, **Doucet**, the **Callot Sisters** followed by **Chanel** and **Poiret**, established their houses in the early decades of the century making Paris the prime centre of fashion. And what they decreed influenced fashion throughout Europe and America. Their ideas were disseminated through illustrated fashion magazines such as *L'Illustration des Modes* and *La Gazette du Bon Ton*, and were slavishly copied by personal dressmakers and by the first ready-to-wear businesses.

For high society women and the aspirant alike fashion shows became a big social event. They were held in the salons of couturiers, at sporting events and in department stores where the new middle classes were able to view cheaper interpretations of Paris couture. The early shows in Paris had none of the chutzpah that is common today. Models, or mannequins as they were known, would walk through the salon in front of seated clients while the couturier pointed out the details of design. Usually drawn from the workshop floor, or found amongst the demi mondaine, the only requirements of a model were slenderness and good manners. She walked rather sedately never uttering a word and never looking directly onto the clients. Couturiers were anxious to distinguish the mannequin from the audience; she was even required to wear a high necked black satin undergarment under the clothes.

The popularity of the fashion shows spread as couturiers became ever more inventive in their self promotion. **Madame Paquin** sent her best looking models to the Longchamp races to show off her designs amongst high society. **Lady Duff Gordon**, an eccentric British couturier behind the couture house of Lucile, trained models to adopt dramatic poses and christened her girls with exotic names, Dinjarzade or Arjamando. But her theatrics backfired, she became known in the trade as Lady Muff Boredom.

'The big american girl' –
the Gibson girl

Dressed by Lucile, Lily Elsie, star
of The Merry Widow, was the figure
of fashion in 1907

In America, the idea of the fashion show was initially treated with great suspicion.

A high society woman, if she was not ordering direct from Paris, preferred to keep the name of her dressmaker private. The taboo was broken during the war. In 1918, the editor of *Vogue*, Edna Woolman Chase, bereft of news from Paris decided to promote New York's home grown talent, according to Seebohm in *The Man Who Was Vogue*, and organised a charity benefit show at The Ritz Carlton hotel. Emily Post, reporting on the event for *Vogue* writes: 'As the procession of mannequins, each announced by Miss Vogue began, a dowager whose own walk sways from side to side but of perfectly sound foundations – watched a particular writhing dipper and fascinated by her collapsing progress she remarked "Mark the model on the programme for me – I think it's too sweet. I am going to get Felice to order one like it for me instead of taking that stodgy old model she wanted me to take." Each woman in the audience delightedly applauded her own dressmaker heart and hand and each had rather a protective feeling toward the Estelle, Mary, or Rose who wore the dresses of the establishment she patronised most and Rose, Mary and Estelle, as they saw the faces of the women before them whom they were accustomed exhibiting gowns, smiled a delighted recognition.'

Modelling was still considered a low class occupation.

The model was stigmatised, as had the artist's model been in centuries before, because she showed her body for a living. Pay was on a par with a salesgirl, and the model's reputation was little better than that of a slut. Couturiers, eager to maintain their own public image, started to pay more attention to the choice of model but they were rarely able to attract the standard of beauty or sophistication they desired.

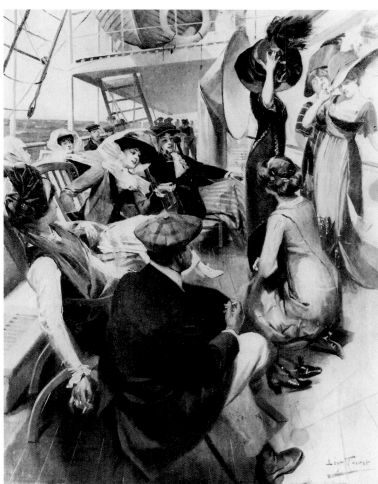

Fashion often exhibited under great difficulties – here models prepare for a show
aboard a liner in 1911

Paul Poiret, and his 'four graces' in London

Denise Poiret, the couturier's wife who was also his first model and muse

Paul Poiret writes despairingly in his diaries *My First Fifty Years* 'The living mannequin is a woman who must be more feminine than all other women. She must react beneath a model, in spirit soar in front of the idea that is being born from her own form, and by her gestures and pose, by the entire expression of her body, she must aid the laborious genesis of the new creation. I have had many mannequins, and very few who were worthy of their priestesshood.' Poiret recalls Andre '...as stupid as a goose, but as beautiful as a peacock...she appeared in my salons like Messalina, like an Indian queen with majestic and haughty pretension, and her sovereign carriage made the authentic princesses before whom she stalked, ponder deeply,' and Yvette '...was one of my stars. She was a little Parisian from Batignolles, with a voice like a pennywhistle. Fortunately her duties did not oblige her to speak' and his favourite, Paulette '...a vapourous blonde, whose pale eyes seemed made of porcelain or glass. With round arms and rounded shoulders she was plump and elegantly rolled as a cigarette.'

'Slim, dark, young, uncorseted, untouched by paint or powder...Mme Poiret is dressed to bring out these features' Poiret wrote of his wife in a 1913 *Vogue*

At home: Denise and Paul Poiret

Mannequins remained a bland bunch until Coco Chanel introduced the idea of the model image. While her contemporaries made do with the girls they could find, **Coco Chanel**, the first truly modern designer was highly selective. Chanel established her name through two shops which she opened between 1912 and 1914 in Deauville and Paris. She started selling millinery, loose blouses and chemises which were notable both for their simplicity and modernity. Chanel's first models were her young aunt Adrienne and Antoinette, her cousin who would parade her latest designs along the promenades of Deauville. They were a striking pair, a perfect advert for Chanel's daring, modern designs and attracted numerous clients. On setting up her *maison de couture* in Paris, Chanel employed full time models. What was unusual about her approach was that she employed them in her own image; demanding strong facial features, a lithe frame and an elegant walk. And if potential models were short on talents, she trained them, rigorously.

Each model had to perfect the 'Coco posture', one foot in front of the other, hips tilted forward, one hand in pocket and the other gesticulating freely. For Chanel, the gesture, the attitude, was all important, it was what gave life to her minimal chic clothes. For society women of the day, accustomed to extravagance and artifice, the cloned image of a strong willed independent woman was some force. And it worked. By the end of the First World War every chic women aspired to be the Chanel woman and every model aspired to be a Chanel model. When it was pointed out that her models were paid notoriously low wages, Chanel asserted: 'They are beautiful girls, let them take lovers'.

Coco Chanel, 1926
Right, Norman Hartnell fashions from 1924

Until the end of the First World War, the model's role remained taboo. Society women and stage stars were the best advertisement for fashion

Georges Lepape's striking cover for Vogue, 1916

Outside of the salon, mannequins found further work posing for illustrators. It was hard work, one single sitting could last for several hours. That many of the leading illustrators of the day were trained artists often made the work creatively torturous. *La Gazette du Bon Ton* and *L'Illustration des Modes* were the leading journals and were particularly inventive in their approach to fashion illustration. Artists were found from Paris' leading college, the Ecole des Beaux Arts, and were encouraged to experiment. The artists, who were practised in drawing from the live model, injected wit and elegance into their work. By comparison, the work of standard illustrators, who relied on photographic portraits for pose and expression, appeared stiff and formulaic.

Styles in illustration moved in tandem with the great artistic movements of the day. Cubism found its expression in lean tubular body shapes, Expressionism in bold blocks of colour while the decorative trends of Art Nouveau and Art Deco were expressed in highly stylised graphic forms which were translated beautifully to the flat magazine page. Until the technology of photography improved, illustrators were the eyes of fashion. Many of the artists who first started working for *La Gazette du Bon Ton* and *L'Illustration*, were later poached by *Vogue* and *Harper's Bazaar*. Here each was encouraged to further devlop their style. In the early years, artist **Helen Dryden**, one of the rare women working in the field, was *Vogue's* main contributor and illustrated many covers.

Georges Lepape, who began working for the couturier, Paul Poiret, introduced a distinctive curvilinear style – his compositions were often undercut with a dose of satire – Spanish born **Edouard Benito** employed a strong and supple line which perfectly suited the gamine, linear fashions of the 1920's while **Paul Iribe**, one of the era's best known illustrators, used bold blocks of colour and clean crisp lines in his highly stylised compositions. It was the illustrators who defined the image of fashionable woman. The most skilled were able to suggest, even through abstract style, the manners and the modes of the time more acutely than any early photographers.

Christian 'Bebé' Bérard, a big, burly flamboyant artist, also a lifelong drug addict, and **Carl Erickson**, an unassuming American with a sharp dry wit, were the two characters of the profession. Bérard was a not only a superb illustrator, he was also an inspiration to the designers, mainly Dior and Schiaparelli. His style was loose, free and passionate. Bettina Ballard, then Paris fashion editor of *Vogue* remembers Bérard in her memoirs *In My Fashion*: 'His face was covered with dabs of paint, a cigarette dangling from his mouth... very occasionally he would look up at the mannequin who was posing in a Lanvin dress in the corner.' Ballard herself later posed for Carl Erickson: 'His drawings never cheated, they showed true elegance when it was there,' writes Ballard, 'and vulgarity even when it might escape the casual eye.'

In the Twenties, illustration was gradually outmoded by photography. But it was some years before the professional model made her debut on the pages of magazines. The first photographic subjects, or the *mannequins du monde* as they became known, were either titled and wealthy women or the actresses and stars of the stage and screen.

Paul Poiret's 'sorbet' dress, 1912, by Georges Lepape

Evening dress by Worth, illustration by Strimpl in
La Gazette du Bon Ton

Georges Barbier's interpretation of Paquin's
pagoda dress from La Gazette du Bon Ton

'Difficult Choice': Evening coat by Worth, drawn
by B.Boutet de Monvel in La Gazette du Bon Ton

In the early years of publication, English and American Vogue carried the same visuals.
A cover from 1917 by Helen Dryden

The influence of Hollywood over fashion grew in the 1930s. The original 'It Girl' make up of arched eyebrows and cupid mouth was set by silent film star Clara Bow

Society
Debutantes and Wives

Ladies,

On the pages of magazines an entirely different breed of model emerged. The *mannequins du monde*, as they became known, were high society women, soubrettes, millionaire wives or the latest rage on stage or screen. They were dressed by couturiers, coerced onto the pages of *Vogue* and *Harpers Bazaar* by debonair photographers, and flattered in society columns. Before the profession of the model became acceptable, the *mannequins du monde* were the face of fashion.

Paris, the reigning city of fashion and culture in the 1920s and 1930s, was home to many fabulous creatures. For the first time, artists, couturiers, actresses and screen stars were permitted into society and in this fertile and highly competitive climate, fashion thrived. And it was the leading figures of this world, of the smart set as it became known, who *Vogue* and *Harpers Bazaar* introduced as the leaders of fashion. Society women exerted great influence; they inspired the work of couturiers and set trends in taste: 'Social standing depended very little on being liked, a weak form of leadership, but rather on the power to make others emulate the way they dressed or entertained or talked and on their ability to make fashionable the people and places they preferred,' writes Bettina Ballard, Paris fashion editor of *Vogue* in her memoirs *In My Fashion*.

The notion of the society model, or *mannequin du monde* had existed for many years. It was common practice for couturiers to offer free clothes in exchange for loyalty and promotion. American socialite Leone Blakemore once asked the couturier Madame Vionnet why her gowns were so reasonably priced; Vionnet replied: 'First I am an artist, and it is a joy to have my work understood and set off to its best advantage, the second is because I am a business woman and you are a good advertisement. I know that when you go to a dinner there will be three women who see you there who will be at my door on Monday asking for the model you wore.'

'I was out every night in every nightclub – seen, seen, seen...'

For the couturiers, society women were an all year round walking advertisement: Constantinople in the Winter, Biarritz in the Summer, Paris for fetes, fashion and grand balls, New York for nightlife and England for country retreats. The society caravan toured the world. And as the years went by the company became increasingly decadent: Diana Vreeland, who was to become *Vogue's* most celebrated fashion editor, writes in her 1984 autobiography *D.V.*: 'I was out every night, in every nightclub – seen, seen, seen – I was always given by the *maison de couture* for being *mannequin du monde* what was known as the *prix jeune fille* – that is to say, they would give me the dress to wear and keep... before the war everyone was dressed by somebody.'

By photographing these beauties, fashion magazines dramatically increased the influence of these women, and that of the couturiers who supplied them with clothes. Initially however, the magazines had a hard time coaxing society ladies onto the pages; posing for a portrait was thought a little close to the trade. Early issues had to make do with snapshots and pithy captions. Stars of the stage and screen were more reliable; daring and provocative, they made perfect models. The dancers of the 1920s proved to be fashion's most glamorous subjects. Gina Palerme, a celebrated French musical comedy star, posed for one remarkably erotic sitting in 1919 wearing a trailing Grecian inspired white Vionnet dress. Josephine Baker, the outrageous Paris-based black performer, caused a stir wherever she appeared: 'Then into our midst walked...Josephine Baker. Now that was historic: we have a black in our house. Her hair had been done by Antoine, the famous hairdresser of Paris, like a Greek Boys – these small flat curls against her skull – she was wearing a white Vionnet dress, cut on the bias with four points, like a handkerchief. It had no opening, no closing...and did Josephine move! These long black legs, these long black arms, this long black throat..and pressed into her flat black curls were white silk butterflies. She had the chic of Gay Paree,' remembers Diana Vreeland in her autobiography.

Diana Vreeland wearing the gown in which she was presented at the Fourth Court of St. James, at Buckingham Palace in May 1933

Oriental fever swept Paris. Lady Lavery, with servant boy at her side, wears an exotic fur-trimmed Poiret coat for a portrait by E.O. Hoppe

As photography improved, images became more
elaborate. The first wave of fashion photographers – **Baron de
Meyer**, **Cecil Beaton** and **Edward Steichen** – used light effects to
dramatise their subjects. Ideas got so out of hand, the publishers of
Vogue and *Harpers Bazaar* Conde Nast and William Hearst, clamped
down on creativity. 'I had mounted a ladder with my camera to
photograph Gertrude Lawrence in a bed as light and airy as
whipped cream,' writes Beaton in his diaries, 'and had remained for
one hour on the ladder exposing dozens of plates while Miss
Lawrence gave a histrionic performance between the flowered
sheets. I was told the photograph was not considered publishable
because in the foreground was a vase of lilies seen out of focus.'

When photographer Paul Tanqueray created a
modernist portrait of Gertrude Lawrence, the judgement was less
harsh. Through the pages of *Vogue* and *Harpers Bazaar*, readers
were exposed to an ever widening circle of notable people. Sarah
Bernhardt, the music hall star (one of the first to licence her name
to beauty products), opera singer Lina Cavlieri and dancer Irene
Castle were amongst the many models. Suzy Solidor, a famous
cabaret star loved by the intellectual circles for her provocative
shows, posed semi naked for photographer Horst, and comedienne
Ina Claire earned her reputation as America's best dressed actress.

As the influence of Hollywood grew over fashion in
the 1930s, magazines turned to cinema stars. *Vanity Fair*, founded
in 1913, became required reading for its ebullient theatre film and
arts coverage. 'Don't stall yourself on life's high road and be
satisfied to take everyone else's dust,' the ad. read. In 1932, Nast
launched *Glamour of Hollywood*, a fashion magazine specifically
dedicated to the silver screen.

The chief influence of Hollywood was over styles in hair and
make up. Actress Clara Bow was the originator of the IT girl make
up; arched eyebrows and cupid mouth, which became the look of
the 1920s, Joan Crawford's rectangular mouth, Jean Harlow's
pencilled eyebrows and Marilyn Monroe's pout set fashions in years
to come. Greta Garbo's enigmatic presence mesmerised readers.
'If our century had entertained a canon of absolute beauty, then this
is it,' declared the photographer, Horst. Both film and television
actresses have continued to exert a powerful influence over fashion.
Mia Farrow, Norma Shearer, Lauren Bacall, Lucile Ball, actually
started their careers as models. The throne of fashion was only
taken away from Hollywood in the late 1980s when the mantle of
fame passed onto the supermodels.

Above, Actresses and dancers injected eroticism into fashion. French
music star Gina Palerme adopts a Venus pose for Vogue in 1919

Right, Josephine Baker the astounding jazz dancer who thrilled high
society in Paris and New York and made black skin fashionable. She
was a favourite mannequin du monde

'Now that was historic: we have a black in our house'

The Six
New Friends
of
Vogue

Françoise

Sophie

Sylvie

Rosine

Toinon

Palmyre

Above, 'The True Exploits of Six Parisiennes, Their Manners and Their Modes', an illustrated series
which was introduced to Vogue in 1922. The beauty in the main photo wears a dress by Dres.
Left, Miss Dorothy Varda in a typical 1920's long neck pose

The beauties of the day were followed around the world. Lady Diana Duff Cooper poses on the deck of a ship leaving New York in 1924

If reluctant to model themselves, society women did concede to pose in fancy dress – costume balls were a favourite form of entertainment in the 1910's and 20s. The Comtesse de Beaumont hosted the era's grandest parties: 'According to Paris gossip the social or artistic value of potential guests was graded as carefully as a stock market report when the Beaumonts compiled the invitation list for their evening parties: where the best of the aristocracy and the best of the artists mixed,' writes Janet Flanner, *The New Yorker* Paris correspondent.

Sartorial competition gave rise to remarkable ingenuity. At the Beaumont's Masterpieces of Painting Ball in 1935, the Baroness of Monaco, aged over 90, appeared as Leonardo da Vinci, for a Futuristic party, society beauty, Marie Laure, dressed up as a squid. *Vogue* gave full page portraits to these remarkable figures. The Texan oil heiress Millicent Rogers posed as Fortune wearing a festooned headress, a hammered satin robe and bearing a glass orb, while the celebrated American hostess, Lady Mendl, formerly Elsie de Wolfe, changed into a Hindu sex goddess.
Editors and photographers were sent *en masse* to cover these splendid occasions. Cecil Beaton describing Lady Erlanger's 1922 ball writes: 'Lady Wimbourne appeared wearing a crinoline of wheat sheaves embroidered in gold. She wagged her hips, pranced about talking common, she shouted to the Duc de Verura "Allo dearie." Mrs Evelyn Fitzgerald glided in wearing a poison green sequinned crinoline. But the best was Princess Baba Lucinge, who really looked the part of water in a flowing armour made of hundreds of strips of tin and a casquette of florin sized sequins.'

As magazines gathered cultural cachet, society women started to appear on pages in couturiers' designs. What they wore and said came to shape a generation's tastes and desires. Millicent Rogers, the Texan oil heiress, was known for her wonderfully eclectic dress sense. She set a fashion for Tyrolean costume and popularised the sculptural designs of couturier Charles James. The 'new dollar princess' as Rogers was known, made the perfect model as her taste was constantly in motion. By contrast, Lady Diana Duff Cooper, wife of Alfred Duff Cooper, a conservative statesman, was revered as a true beauty. 'Her face was perfect oval, her skin white marble, her lips japonica red, her hair flaxen, her eyes blue love in the mist,' wrote Beaton.

Above, Millicent Rogers, oil heiress, as she appeared in 1924 dressed for a costume ball

Left, Modelling was a very fashionable pursuit: Mrs Christabel Russell at the Daily Mirror Fashion Fair held at Holland Park Hall in 1923

Just one day prior to the historic wedding, Wallis Simpson in the grounds of Château de Cande, 1937 by Cecil Beaton for Vogue

American socialites, less shy of publicity, were frequent subjects. Lady Mendl, wife of Sir Charles Mendl, a press attaché to the British Embassy and reputedly the first female interior designer, promoted her talents through her magazine appearances. She cultivated pet eccentricities. 'Lady Mendl was famous for standing on her head every morning for preserving her youthful figure, she had an abrupt and abrasive wit and a candid dislike for failure and sickness,' said photographer Hoyningen-Huene. The Honourable Mrs.Reginald Fellowes, millionaire heiress, was another trendsetter. Couturiers of the day courted the era's beauties, even mixing in the same elite circles. Russian born Lady Abdy, who worked as a model for Chanel, popularised the designers' modern chic designs amongst the Parisian intellectual set. Her characteristic coiffure of two macaroons of hair behind each ear was much imitated.

Coco Chanel in 1929 with her model and friend Lady Abdy who launched a fad for 'macaroon' hairstyles

The lady of the Brobdingnagian bangles: Nancy Cunard in 1932

Photographic styles
changed with fashion.
Gertrude Lawrence as
the modernist by Paul
Tanqueray for Vogue

It was not only physical presence of the era's beauties which fascinated, readers became obsessed with the minute details of their glamorous lives.

The appetite for fashion trivia remained unequalled until the supermodels arrived on the scene in the late 1980s. Readers learnt of the seven daschunds which Mrs. Fellowes carried on her travels, of Lady Mendl's habit of taking twenty pairs of white gloves to an evening soiree; as soon as one pair was stained she changed. The aristocratic beauty, Rita Lydig, was known to own 150 pairs of handmade lace shoes; Millicent Rogers was apt to change her outfit up to three times during one evening. As Janet Flanner remarked, people were some people in those years.

The unofficial models reigned over fashion for thirty years

and via the first mass circulation magazines transformed the elite world of couture into a public sport. Between the years of 1909 and 1938 *Vogue's* circulation jumped from 14,000 to 138,000 with *Harpers Bazaar* not far behind. The magazine industry boomed, *Femina*, *Good Housekeeping*, *Glamour*, and *Tatler* grew to appeal to the ever widening band of fashion consumers. As the appetite for fashion increased, the professional model was soon in demand.

Above, Hoyningen-Huene captures Madame Lelong (wife of couturier Lucien Lelong, formerly Princess Natalie Paley) in a wistful moment. Here she wears a dress designed by her husband, in Vogue 1931

Right, a sun hat on the Riviera: Lady Abdy by George Hoyningen-Huene for Vogue 1932

► END

Fashion
Photo

Harrods' Younger Set Departments

2. Sophisticated schoolgirl—in navy blue crêpe, a spotless expanse of collar highlighting the fine pleated bodice; easy skirt. 8 gns., Trayles

3. First prize for neatness—Matita's navy wool dress with slim white neckband, slim pair of belts, tucked diaphragm. 6½ guineas, Fenwick

4. Young, beguiling—Susan Small's romaine dress has a taffeta apron round its middle, a childish piqué collar. 5½ gns., Dickins and Jones

5. Shining as soapsuds—the piqué accents, the spanking white buttons on Matita's snug bolero over a navy wool dress. 8½ guineas, Hamilton

The main springboard for change in the status of the model was the advancement in fashion photography

graphy

During the roaring Twenties, modelling became fashionable. As class prejudices broke down, titled women started to appear on magazines pages, and a handful of professional models were accepted into the hub of society. 'Even if you had been working like mad you would rush home in the evening and dress yourself up and I really mean dress up, in lace, jewels, all sorts of hats; you had to have so many hats then – I remember my favourite was a little skull cap with diamond clips – and gloves, you always wore gloves,' said Chanel's prized model, Toto Koopman (left), 'Everyone went out in the evenings, there was always a place to be seen at. We were all exhibitionists, show offs – one dressed up not to please men but to astound other women.'

The main springboard for change in the status of the model was photography. By mid decade, photography had replaced illustration as the chief visual medium in magazines and, in number or in beauty, there were insufficient society ladies to fill the pages. To keep impetus, fashion magazines constantly needed to redefine the fashion image and it was the need for change which created the genre of fashion photography and so introduced the model to the magazine page: 'A picture editor or art director on a magazine is faced with having to tell the same story year after year and all he has to present are photographs of the newest fashions,' wrote Conde Nast in a memo to *Vogue's* art director Heyworth Campbell (recorded in *The Man Who Was Vogue* by Caroline Seebohm) 'To make the page appear different he has to secure variety somehow.' In the 1920s and 1930s, fashion photography was wildly experimental. There was no precedent; photographers, some of whom were trained artists, interpreted with a free hand and the competition between the two leading titles, *Harper's Bazaar* and *Vogue*, further encouraged invention. It was on the pages of these 'quality glossies' that creative fashion photography was founded: '...from the moment photographers' preoccupations moved to the pose and expression of their models, they exceeded the brief of providing a record, an illustration,' writes Martin Harrison in his history of fashion photography *Appearances*, 'Fashion photography began to appreciate that it could comment on, as well as reflect, its subject matter.' Photographers helped to find models, and directed their own shoots, there was none of the formality of today. Stylistic inspiration came from greater artistic movements – during those early years the influence of Art Deco, Art Nouveau, Surrealism all found expression in the fashion image.

The first models tended to be adventurous women or women who were attracted by the artistry of photography; posing was still considered fast and loose: 'In Montparnasse, we were all friends, and modelling was for camaraderie, you know, for pleasure more than anything else,' said Jacqueline Goddard, a favourite of Man Ray, 'Half of the photos which were made of me, were done for nothing...it was just a period when people seemed to have their noses just above water, everybody was struggling.'

Lisa Fonssagrives was a talented ballet dancer and also choreographer. Her enigmatic beauty, and perfectly controlled posture made her one of the most revered models of all time. She was photographed by the pioneers: Horst, Man Ray and Erwin Blumenfeld and later became the adored subject of her husband, Irving Penn. 'It's not that Lisa produces an effect in the pictures,' Penn once said, 'That is what she is.' Fonssagrives' feats included parachuting for Jean Moral and hanging from the Eiffel tower for Erwin Blumenfeld. **Marion Morehouse**, the archetypal flapper girl, was discovered on New York's social scene, while fellow New Yorker, **Lee Miller**, escaped to Paris with dreams of becoming an artist, when she started modelling. Chanel's prized model, **Toto Koopman**, who later worked with Hoyningen-Huene was one of the few who crossed over from a couture house.

Vogue's **first full-time** fashion photographer **Baron de Meyer**, who was paid a princely $100 a week, was the first photographer to set a style. He managed to turn the plainest of subjects into magical beauties through the use of haloed light effects and decorative props. In 1922 de Meyer, in the first of many poaches between the two leading fashion magazines, was lured onto *Harper's Bazaar*. Later in the decade, his style became sadly outdated. Fashion was changing; the new school of couturiers, led by Chanel, were working with simple, sporty streamlined designs and there was no place for de Meyer's romantic view of women.

Nast found his next recruit in the young **Edward Steichen**, whose clean images suited the go ahead 1920s: 'Every woman in de Meyer's photograph looks like a model,' said Nast to Steichen, 'You make every model look like a woman.' It was Steichen's work with **Marion Morehouse** that revolutionised the fashion image. She was the first in a long line of models, including Barbara Goalen in the 1950s, Twiggy in the 1960s and Lauren Hutton in the 1970s, who set a standard of beauty. Morehouse with her boyish figure, long neck was the archetypal flapper girl: 'Miss Morehouse was no more interested in clothes than I was,' writes Steichen in his memoirs, 'But when she put on the clothes that were to be photographed, she transformed herself into a woman who really would wear that gown or riding habit or whatever it was.'

Steichen repeatedly photographed Morehouse, and caught her self reliant attitude and flirty poses in disarmingly real photographs. When magazines became increasingly commercial during the 1930s, Steichen, disillusioned, retired from fashion photography. Morehouse went on to marry the experimental poet e.e.Cummings. Steichen's assistant, a Baltic baron by the name of George Hoyningen-Huene, succeeded the *Vogue* throne. Whereas Steichen had realised the modern woman, Hoyningen-Huene became synonymous with the classical siren of the 1930s. Models in Hoyningen-Huene's images appeared elegant and serene; their personality was never revealed – gesture, composition and lighting, were attuned to the ideal.

Edward Steichen

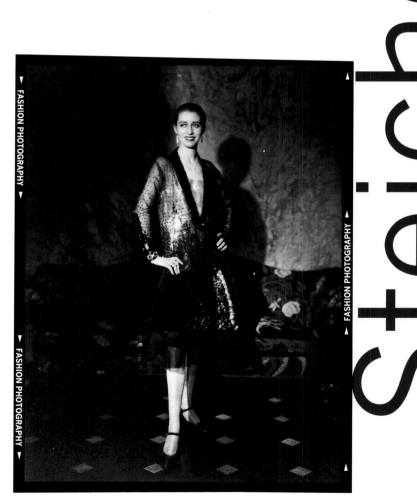

FASHION PHOTOGRAPHY

FASHION PHOTOGRAPHY

Above, Marion Morehouse: the archetypal flapper girl, Vogue, 1927

Right, 'The Victorious Wreath' by Edward Steichen for Vogue, 1932

The artist and photographer Man Ray, a contributor to *Harper's Bazaar*, was the wittiest and most inventive photographer of the era. He was the first to initiate the use of the mechanical airbrush, and produced a cameraless photography that produced images which he called Rayographs. Man Ray always followed his own agenda which was heavily influenced by the Surrealists. His models appeared expressionless and vacant, an illusion which was enhanced by solarisation – a technique which gives an eerie, silvery cast. Through his various technical conjuring tricks, Man Ray was able to satirise much of the inevitable frivolity of fashion. Photography, he believed, was the medium of fantasy: 'I paint what I cannot photograph,' he was to declare, 'I photograph what I cannot paint.'

He worked with a number of models. Kiki de Montparnasse, Man Ray's lover of the early Twenties, was by far his most photographed subject. For fashion work, **Lee Miller**, a gamine blonde, his lover and also assistant, was Man Ray's favourite. Miller, a true chameleon model, was the darling of many. She posed for Horst, Steichen, Hoyningen-Huene, and later was to become an accomplished photographer in her own right: 'I really was terribly, terribly pretty,' Lee Miller once said, 'I looked like an angel, but I was a fiend inside.'

Above, Kiki de Montparnasse: the woman who introduced Man Ray to Bohemian cafe society

Left, Lee Miller in a strikingly modern pose, an example of Man Ray's use of the technique of solarisation

The haughty sophisticate replaced the spirited flapper girl in the 1930s. A Schiaparelli suit by Horst for Vogue

Horst P. Horst

More romantic than Hoyningen-Huene and more flamboyant than Steichen, **Horst P. Horst** introduced a sense of life and volume into the fashion image. His models simply had presence. Horst, a one time assistant to Hoyningen-Huene went through many stylistic shifts. He started his career photographing lily-skinned beauties in classical poses, the influence of Surrealism took him in another direction. Models who were more idiosyncratic in their features, appeared in tableau sets propped with plaster casts and surrealist symbols. 'Before the war, Paris was the cultural elegance centre of the world. And the nice thing about Paris was that everybody was mixed up together; princes, writers, painters were all friends,' said Horst in an interview with *Vogue* in the late 1980s. 'There was no separation as today. Today it's money.'

Erwin **Blumenfeld**

Lisa Fonssagrives on the Eiffel Tower wearing a Lucien Lelong dress, French Vogue, 1939

Louise Dahl
Above, A typical outdoor-girl shot by Louise Dahl-Wolfe for Harper's Bazaar

Wolfe

By the mid Thirties, the model had witnessed numerous transformations from romantic ideal, to flapper, to Greek goddess and modern siren. Photographic styles had influenced fashion so much that in 1933, records Seebohm, *Vogue's* sister publication, *Vanity Fair,* was able to pastiche the fashion shoot. The series, shot by Hoyningen-Huene with the same model, aped de Meyer, Cecil Beaton and Steichen. It begged the question whether fashion photography was forgetting the woman, for the sake of art.

The Rolliflex camera, and colour film, introduced new levels of reality into the fashion picture; photographers were able to capture movement, the colour of skin and the pattern of clothes. For the first time the model could be photographed outdoors. American photographers were pioneers. Free from the artistic pretension and bourgeois tradition of Europe, the fresh air school, as it became known, was inspired by homegrown beauty. Suddenly the model was seen to live and breathe and move.

Harpers Bazaar's fashion editor from 1932, Carmel Snow, was to launch the action fashion shot. She signed up a Hungarian sports photographer **Martin Munkacsi**. The timing was perfect, swimming, golf, diving were fashionable pastimes, and simple lively images were much needed in a time of depression. Along with Munkacsi, came a new breed of sporty atheletic models. His favourite was Lucile Brokaw. Carmel Snow says in her memoirs: 'Munkacsi wanted the model to run toward him. Such a pose had never been attempted before – fashion even sailing features were posed in a studio on a fake boat – but Lucile was certainly game and so was I. The resulting picture of a typical American girl in action with her cape billowing behind her, made photographic history.' Brokaw was the first healthy all-American outdoor model and blueprint for a type of model including Lauren Hutton and Patti Hansen in the 1970s, and Bridget Hall in the 1990s, who became known as outdoor girls. As with Brokaw, the outdoor girl image became a staple for fashion in times of economic uncertainty. Honest, healthy faces could sell fashion in tough times.

In Munkacsi's wake came Louise Dahl-Wolfe and Toni Frissell who developed the ideal of the natural woman. Louise Dahl-Wolfe, who worked for *Harper's Bazaar* between 1935 and 1958, made the all-American healthy outdoor look her personal forté, communicating directly with her models and making them feel at ease: 'I adored posing for her,' said one of her favourites, Liz Gibbons, 'her running praises were head-turning and believable.' Toni Frissell, a former debutante, started off her career as a society snapper and journalist for American *Vogue*. She was first hired as a fashion photographer in the inaugural years of *Life* magazine and her reputation later led to work for *Harper's Bazaar*. Frissell tacked into the spirit of female liberation expressing the ideal through a style of photo reportage. Her images embodied the vibrant, sporty modern woman. She produced probably the first photograph of a woman wearing a bikini, with long long legs stretching into the foreground, which perfectly summed up the era's new found freedom. It was through the pioneering work of the first generation of fashion photographers that the fashion model transformed from a characterless nobody and came to be seen as an ideal of her times.

In the 1930s a supple figure and a suntan were the best accessories of fashion, by Anton Bruehl in Vogue, 1937

FASHION PHOTOGRAPHY

The first colour cover was shot by Edward Steichen for Vogue in 1932

VOGUE

BEAU
NUMB
JULY 1, 1
PRICE 35

©THE CONDE
PUBLICATION

The fresh air school were American based. Free of the artistic pretension and bourgeois tradition of Europe, they were inspired by homegrown beauty

Toni Frissell for US Vogue, 1937

Vogue
INCORPORATING VANITY FAIR

The glamourous fashion world portrayed in the magazines attracted unequalled interest in the 1920s and the promise of glamour and travel began to attract more well-bred girls to modelling. In 1924, the Parisian couturier Jean Patou advertised for fashion models to show his collection in New York, realising his own Paris girls were too short on the leg and too exotic looking to appeal to American clients who were used to a leaner, healthier ideal. In the advertisement he requested smart and slender models, '...with well shaped feet and ankles and a refined manner.'

Over 500 applicants replied, the quality of candidates was surprisingly high. **Hannah Lee Stokes**, the daughter of a lawyer's family in Boston, was one of the five selected along with **Edwina Prue**, a tall Texan beauty. Stokes, lured by the chance of adventure and wealth answered the ad and worked for Patou for nine months, travelling to Paris after the American tour. On her return to New York, she was greeted as a minor celebrity and soon found lucrative advertising work. Stokes' reception was a sign that the market was rapidly changing. The booming fashion and advertising agencies wanted pretty girls to promote their products, the manufacturers required models to sell clothing to buyers, the growing magazine market needed models to pose for illustrators and photographers, and the cosmetic industry, faces to sell its products. It was not long before entrepreneurs realised there was money in modelling. This was the start of the model agency business, a history which was recorded in detail in Michael Gross' 1995 book *Model: the Ugly Business of Beautiful Women*.

John Robert Powers, an out of work actor, opened the first model agency in New York in 1923. The operation was basic. According to Gross, Powers gathered together his actor and actress friends, a list of fashion houses and advertising businesses, and sent them out with a sheet of addresses to pound the pavements. Bookings started to come in, the service answered a need. Much of the work was mundane, but the pay, averaging around $5 an hour was reasonable. Department stores such as Henri Bendel and Bergdorf Goodman provided reliable work modelling in fashion shows which had become a regular fixture. There was very little glamour attached to the job; outside of show hours, models would also be expected to dress windows, sell clothes and tidy up after a day's trading. For the majority of clients as long as a girl was slim, healthy and pretty and could walk in a straight line and show a certain amount of flare, then she had the potential to model. Only *Vogue* and *Harper's Bazaar* judged by aesthetics, and these were the rare cachet jobs.

For the general public, the word model still implied a woman of low repute, a show girl or a prostitute. In fact the stigma attached to the word was so great that Powers avoided it altogether and instead used 'Powers Girls' describing his models as 'Long Stemmed American Beauties.' He even provided them with hat boxes to carry on the street stamped with the agency's name, which helped promote the business and add pzazz to the image. The calibre of girls Powers was able to attract altered dramatically after the Wall Street crash of 1929. Lure of money clearly won out over prejudice. Debutante daughters signed up on the books, society women began to dabble; suddenly respectable parents and husbands were more than happy to see their loved ones pasted up on billboards for a suitable sum. Modelling also proved a useful stepping stone into marriage or into Hollywood. Film stars including Lucille Ball, Ava Gardner, Lauren Bacall and Norma Shearer were some of the many that passed through the agency's hands.

Lucie Clayton and some of her model girls, 1946

Learning the tricks of the trade at the Mayfair School in New York

A spectacular outdoor fashion show at Selfridge's department store, London

In Europe, a different type of model agency was established in the charm school. **Lucie Clayton's** in London was the first to open in 1928. The school, whose alumni include Jean Shrimpton and Celia Hammond, was founded by Sylvia Gollidge, a former department store model from Blackpool. As in America, prejudice still ran high. To make the business sound reputable, Gollidge changed her name to the respectable Lucie Clayton, and promoted the agency as a charm school. Unlike Powers, Gollidge charged the girls, or their parents, fees. In return she taught deportment, basic elocution, and social manners. As the girls were paying, there were no restrictions on entry. Gollidge's promised to transform any young girl, whether dumpy, skinny or socially inept, into a lady. The class ridden society of 1930s England made Lucie Clayton's enterprise an immediate success. If a woman was to become a successful model, she required the affectations of class and style, and Gollidge provided the tricks and the publicity. During the depression in the 1930s, Gollidge recruited six girls from improverished South Wales coal-mining communities, offered them free tutoring and packed them off to Hollywood on a highly publicised touring fashion show which was sponsored by British clothing manufacturers. Lucie Clayton's coming out day became a stock story for newspapers. By 1950 Slyvia Gollidge was able to retire to Australia with the £2,200 earnt from the sale of her agency. During the 1930s charm schools sprung up throughout Europe and America. Methods of tuition varied, and the Americans were particularly innovative. The **Mayfair School** in New York used three foot high wooden mannequins, complete with painted eyelashes, toenails and nipples, to teach its students how to pose. Mayfair girls also learnt the art of 'speed' dressing which involved pulling dress after dress on and off over fancy hairstyles while the mistress of the school watched on with a stopwatch and clipboard. The first charm schools and agencies not only simplified the booking of models, they helped to upgrade the image of the profession. And as the agency business grew, the quality of models improved.

In 1946, former model, **Eileen Ford**, set up what was to become the most famous agency – **Ford Models**. The agency offered career training and professional advice. Ford started her business as a p.a. to a Swedish model called Natalie Lindgren, and soon attracted top flight girls from the big Powers and Conover agencies. With her special breed of hands-on management, Ford turned modelling into a career, and the model agency into an influential power monger. No longer were girls merely booked for a job, they were nurtured; Ford offered models beds in her family home, groomed, packaged and offered them to the right client at the right time. Agency and client were placed on equal footing, and woe betide any photographer who messed with a Ford model, never would he be allowed to book through the agency again. The Ford Agency, which now expands to offices in Paris, Miami and Brazil with a turnover which reaches into the multi-millions, marked the start of what has become a highly lucrative and cut-throat business.

The grim years of the depression which swept through America and Europe in the 1930s forced magazines and couturiers to take a more realistic approach. Along with the fantastical and creative, straightforward and practical fashion photography was introduced, featuring healthy bright women in plain cost-effective clothing which could be interpreted at little cost by the readers.

The Second World War temporarily halted experiment. Although some couturiers continued to design during the war it was for the *souris gris*, the grey mice wives of the Nazi officers. The fashion industry effectivly closed down, there was no news from Paris until 1944. One of the very last fashion shoots before the occupation by Andre Durst in 1940 is a prophetic image of models seated on packing cases in the hallway of a couturiers salon. It was a farewell salute to the pioneering 1930s.

Cecil Beaton and Lee Miller continued to work during the war, social editors spent their evenings chatting to high society in air raid shelters, and fashion editors championed the enterprising efforts of women who, against all odds, managed to keep up appearances. Horst was recruited to the army, Lee Miller travelled Europe documenting the horrors of war, society beauty Lady Diana Duff Cooper managed farms. Fonssagrives, Man Ray, Hoyningen-Huene emigrated to New York where without directives from Paris, a new homegrown fashion industry started to blossom. After liberation, the focus moved back to Paris when the gloom and the shockof the war years was finally lifted by Christain Dior's triumphant New Look collection of 1947.

Cecil Beaton and Lee Miller continued to work during the war, Horst was recruited to the army, Lee Miller travelled Europe documenting the horrors of war, Fonssagrives, Hoyningen-Huene emigrated to New York

**From Utility severity, above, Vogue 1939
to celebrating victory, left, Vogue 1944**

► END

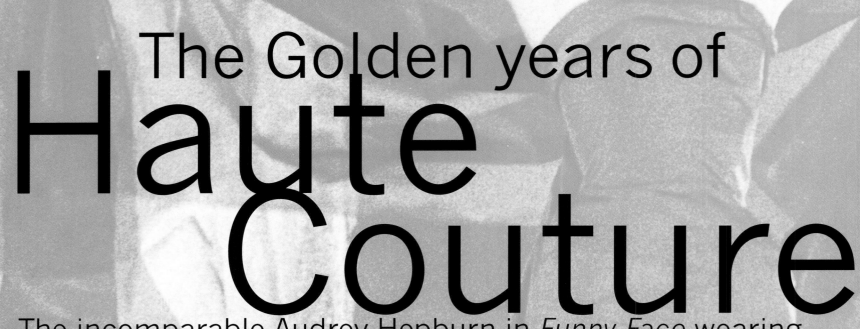

The Golden years of
Haute
Couture

The incomparable Audrey Hepburn in *Funny Face* wearing Givenchy. Inset, a model makes an entrance at Dior, 1955

The model was made a symbol in the 1950s not merely a useful prop, but the centrepiece and the public image of fashion. The era saw the first star models, Lisa Fonssagrives, Suzy Parker, Barbara Goalen, Fiona Campbell-Walter and Dorian Leigh, daily newspapers started to carry model stories, and by 1957 the model world was so familiar it could be sent up in the film *Funny Face*. *Vogue* ran its first model competition:
'You can reassure your father, your husband and your son, on one point: modelling is terribly respectable,' it read.

It was the increasingly commercial fashion industry of the 1950s which afforded the model fame and respect. Fashion was no longer seen as the preserve of an elite, magazines and the booming ready-to-wear industry introduced fashion into the life of every woman. Paris couturiers set the trends, newspapers relayed the news and magazines added gloss to the image and mass manufacturers followed suit. The model was essential to the process. Couturiers could no longer rely on a rag bag of girls to sell their clothes, they needed showmanship, style and likewise neither could magazines afford to present fashion through photographers' artistic pictures of their friends. Fashion needed an **ideal**, an aspirational model who could appeal across any national and class boundaries – a woman of the world. Both the catwalk show and the photographic image changed drastically.

Christian Dior changed the format of the show in his legendary collection of 1947 **The New Look**:

'I was conscious of an electric tension which I had never before felt in couture...the first girl came out stepping fast, twitching with a provocative swinging movement, whirling in the close packed room, knocking over ashtrays with the strong flare of her pleated skirts and bringing everyone to the edges of their seats in a desire not to miss the thread of this momentous occasion. . . we were given a polished theatrical performance such as we had never seen in a couture house before. We were witness to a revolution in fashion and to a revolution in showing fashion as well,' writes *Vogue* fashion editor Bettina Ballard in her memoirs.

Dior made his models perform, live the image of the clothes rather than simply show cut and cloth. Between 1947 and his death in 1958 Dior ruled fashion, he sold more than one and half time the clothes than fellow Paris couturiers put together. Each season he introduced a totally new silhouette, including the H Line, the I line and the Trapeze line, and his models attuned their poses and attitude to the shape and feel of each collection.

The New Look silhouette and the new look model: Haughty, proud and sophisticated. The ballet dancer's pose which exaggerated the nipped in, hourglass shape, became a standard of the era

We were witness to a **revolution** in fashion and to a revolution in showing fashion as well

Left, 'The world is a hard place; women must be the smile of the world,' said Christian Dior. He preferred his models soft, feminine with plump cheeks, and smiling, above all smiling

Right, Fashion's master photographer, Richard Avedon, takes a front row pew at the Paris collections, next to Carmel Snow, right, fashion editor of Harper's Bazaar

Left, Setting the foundations of modern fashion: a lean figure and slimming underwear

Right, Modelling became respectable and women from America and Europe descended on Paris to live and work

A model shows a fluted
peplum suit, a success
from Balenciaga 1950.
The master of purity
hated publicity and had
little time for 'star'
models

Competition forced each couturier to develop a type of model. Although the variants

stretched little further than vamp, woman of the world, and young go ahead woman there were distinguishing traits and faces. **Givenchy** favoured small boned gamine types to show his youthful fashion, the ideal was found in Audrey Hepburn. Balmain mixed young cocottes with women of the world, **Balenciaga** preferred plain models to set of the purity and line of his architectural designs.

Where in the pre-war years the work and employment

of the salon models had been ad hoc, in the 1950s the model role was made formal. Each couturier employed what was known as a *cabine* which comprised a group of between 7 and 12 models who would work everyday while the collection was prepared. After the show they continued to work for another two weeks, posing for the photographers and illustrators in the morning, and then modelling the collection for the buyers in the afternoon. The hours were very long and unremitting: 'I was surprised when I was shown where the mannequins had to clock in in the morning, just like all the other employees at Dior. If one arrived after 9am it was marked in red and meant deduction from one's pay,' writes Jean Dawnay in her memoirs *Model Girl,* 1956. Each of the models would be fitted, pinned and draped with cloth day in day out, until a satisfactory design was conceived and the harder the model would work to inspire the couturier, the more designs were created for her. As each outfit reached completion, a ribbon or tape bearing the model's name would be sewn into the inside seam.
Favourite models, the ones who attracted the greatest number of orders, would be asked back season after season. They became known as 'house' models, their tenure stretching up to ten years.

The vendeuse was the couturier's right hand, responsible for selling the collection and vetting prospective models

Competition forced each couturier
to develop
a type of
model

Oriental models were adored for their femininity and grace. Hiroko Matsumoto, above, was one of a handful including China Machado at Givenchy and Alla at Dior; Matsumoto became Pierre Cardin's muse in 1957

Pierre Balmain's house models were actressy girls who made headlines. The most famous was a Welsh model, **Bronwen Pugh,** who made the pages of *The New York Times* when she dragged a fur coat along the aisle. Her impudence shocked the genteel clientele of the house. Dior always preferred exoticism to drama and his favourite was **Alla**, a half Russian Manchu model and one of the earliest Asian models: 'She is a natural born model...while Alla's face has all the mysterious charm of the East, she is still half Russian. As a result she has a perfectly European body and I know that any woman who chooses a design she has worn will not be disappointed,' writes Dior in his memoirs. Alla became the ambassador for Dior on trips abroad, she was photographed by Avedon and Louis Dahl-Wolfe and continued to model for the house of Dior when Yves Saint Laurent was appointed head designer after Dior's death in 1957.

After closing her salon in 1939, Coco Chanel made her comeback in 1954. She reformed her cabine of girls; all her models, slim and assured continued the tradition that Chanel had originally established in the 1920's. Marie-Helene Arnaud headed up the cabine and after Chanel's death took over the running of the salon. Florida born model, Eugenia McLin, worked as a house model for Chanel for over six years.
'Chanel was terrifying, she controlled everything, I think all the models were scared of her. I would work every day for fittings, it was arduous work, she was a perfectionist through and through. It was good money, about $400 a month and at the end of the season we would be given two or three outfits; the models were allowed to buy the fabric at wholesale cost. One day, Chanel decided she did not like the way I smiled, and she fired me.'

'She possessed a tragic beauty' writes Pierre Balmain of Bronwen Pugh (below) in his memoirs

Above, 'All my designs represent a vicarious love affair with women whose beauty I delight in enhancing'said US couturier, Charles James

Left, In the post-war years fashion shows went on tour. At the Savoy Hotel 1951, 22 couturiers showed their collections

Money as well as fame encouraged models to make a performance. On top of the statutory cabine fee, some houses paid a percentage of the designs sold. House models showed anything up to sixteen outfits, elaborate expensive designs made to appeal to couturier's celebrity clients. 'Bread and butter' models showed plainer designs which were ordered by conservative clients. Each cabine, was kept in order by the chief vendeuse, and had its own jokes and rituals. If the name of the model did not suit, it was changed in a ritual called a baptism. The daughter of a bus driver, Janine, was named Praline at Balmain, Simone Bodin became **Bettina**, and Germaine Lefèvre, **Capucine** at Givenchy.

An air of good breeding was essential to the 1950's model girl. Two models pose in fairytale gowns by Hardy Amies, couturier to the Royal Family

Capucine

The icy beauty Capucine 'Cap' was renowned for her humour while copper haired and freckled faced Bettina hit headlines when she got involved with the millionaire Aly Khan

Bettina

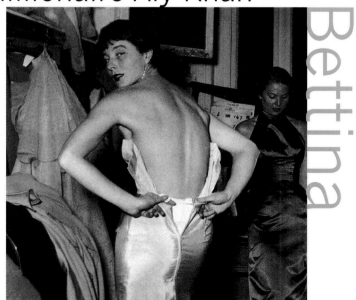

The fashion show became a novel parade. In 1954 designers staged a show in a Chipperfield circus tent pitched on Blackheath

Schiaparelli fur and Ottman silk evening dress modelled in a notably relaxed pose

Above, Model girls on tour

Right, Texan born Suzy Parker, who started modelling aged 14, was the glamour model of the 1950s

During the 1950s

Show models and photographic models were two different breeds; show models were not necessarily beautiful, the basic requirements were a lean trim figure and a graceful walk, photographic models needed large eyes, good bones and translucent skin. During the decade, as modelling became a respectable profession, it was the photographic models who first courted fame.

The beauties of the day

were Suzy Parker, Dovima, Lisa Fonssagrives, Anne Gunning, Dorian Leigh and the impossibly elegant Barbara Goalen. Each model was shaped and nurtured by a photographer: Parker by Avedon; Fonssagrives by her husband Irving Penn; Anne Gunning, Richard Dormer; Barbara Goalen by John French. The duos were as famous as Bailey and Shrimpton, Linda Evangelista and Steven Meisel were in years to come. These close-knit photographer-and-model relationships produced the most memorable fashion images of the era. And there were many. Fashion photographers, reacting against the rigid and humourless style of the 1940s, scaled new heights of eloquence and elegance.

Irving Penn

brought great dignity to fashion photography. He reduced the image to its essence, often shooting his models in graphic silhouette against plain white backgrounds:
'I don't think the girl's personality should ever intrude, (sic: who the model) was as a real person was not of any significance,' he once said. His beloved subject was his wife Lisa Fonssagrives, the dancer who modelled for Blumenfeld and Horst in the pre war years. Through Penn's lens, Fonssagrives was made an icon of pure elegance: serene, beautiful and knowing. Images such as *Harlequin Dress* (*Vogue,* 1950) in which Fonssagrives poses nonchalantly under a tricorn hat, cigarette in hand and *Mermaid Dress* of the same year, in which Fonssagrives' body is seen to echo the shape of an upturned champagne flute are classic masterpieces of fashion photography. In 1950 Penn completed a landmark fashion shoot for American *Vogue*. For its elegance and poignancy, the series, shot against simple white background, became a pointer against which all future fashion photographs would be measured:

'The best

of the earlier work – by de Meyer, Steichen, Beaton, Hoyningen Huene and others – now seems close to theatre, with the dress and its model playing a role. But Penn's 1950 pictures provide no references to plot or circumstance, no suggestions of old chateaux, or perfect picnics, of delicious flirtations in Edwardian dining rooms...They are not stories, but simply pictures,' writes the photographic historian John Szarkowski in Irving Penn's 1984 monograph. Penn's images were so intense and incisive, *Vogue* readers complained. The publication took note and reduced his allocation of pages, but Penn refused to compromise.

Barbara Goalen (left) nicknamed 'The-Got-It-Girl' or 'La Goalen' and Fiona Campbell-Walter epitomized the England of stately homes. Well bred manners and stylized elegance helped raise the profile of the modelling profession

It was in the 1950s that another great photographer **Richard Avedon** first made his mark. By contrast to Penn, asserts Martin Harrison in *Appearances*, Avedon sought to capture a sense of energy and real life. In terms of style, his work continued the real life vein which photographers Louise Dahl, Wolfe and Martin Munkasci established in the late 1930s. Models ran, lived and breathed in his images; they express a carefree exuberance and a great love of life. Avedon paid enormous attention to his choice of model; he believed gesture and movement best evoked the spirit of the times. He preferred actressy types and in the early part of the decade, Dorian Leigh was Avedon's reigning model, followed by the very glamorous Suzy Parker, Leigh's sister, and the raven headed Dovima. Twiggy, Penelope Tree and Lauren Hutton were his favourites through the 1960s.

Many of Avedon's fashion photographs have become classics of the genre. *Dovima and The Elephants* (1955) in which a femme fatale is flanked by preposterously large elephants, is an acute summation of the grand splendour of era. Later into the decade, Avedon changed to a semi documentary style in which his models really did 'act.' In one legendary shoot for US *Vogue* in 1962 Suzy Parker appears as Elizabeth Taylor in a narrative story based on the actress's notorious affair with Richard Burton (in Avedon's story played by Mike Nichols). One shot shows Parker leaving a hospital with her hand in bandages, supposedly after an attempted suicide. The image caused an uproar. Throughout his long career Avedon, arguably the greatest fashion photographer ever, has continued to redefine and reinvent the fashion image. And it is through his lens, that some of fashion's greatest models emerged.

In England, **John French**'s exquisitely elegant images for the *Daily Express*, revolutionised fashion in newspapers. Every model appeared well bred and supremely feminine. Modelling becoming an acceptable profession was largely due to French, and through the years readers were introduced to many of fashion's faces: Shelagh Wilson, Jennifer Hocking, Rosalind Watkins and Jean Dawnay amongst. French's celebrated model was Barbara Goalen, or 'La Goalen' as she became known. She was the embodiment of the England of stately homes and Belgravia; the clothes she wore looked like her own. Women not only aspired to own the clothes Goalen wore, they wanted to be her: 'They were vintage years. One was treated like the queen. We were taken everywhere in a chauffeur driven Rolls. I loved every minute of it,' Goalen once said. A *Vogue* photographer, **Henry Clarke**, who worked with Dovima, Parker, Fonssagrives and others, was, like French, gentlemanly in his approach. He captured grace and femininity.

The model emerged as a glamorous and knowing figure in the 1950s; a woman of the world. A repertoire of poses was developed; a static hand on hips pose with feet placed in a ballet dancer's fifth position as a standard (the nipped waist corsetted designs allowed for little movement). It was through the eyes, made up with a sleek cat's eye line of kohl, and hand gestures that models learnt to express well bred elegance. The high stylized image proved utterly desirable. For the first time modelling was seen as aspirational; women slavishly copied the hair styles and gestures of La Goalen, Parker and Dorian Leigh.

Above, Dorian Leigh in Paris. Leigh founded the first modelling agency in Paris in the late 1950s

Right, Fiona Campbell-Walter, high society girl, prepares for a show at Alexander's department store, New York

'The dollar a minute girl', Dovima represented the 50's ideal of elegance. She was the daughter of a Polish cop from Queens

The models were the
glamourous most
desired
women of the era

Newspapers made model stories a regular fixture. There was plenty to report; the era's beauties were courted by the titled and rich: Fiona Campbell-Walter married German millionaire, Baron von Thyssen, making headline news; Bronwen Pugh, who was reputedly discovered on Basingstoke railway station, married Lord Astor; Anne Cumming-Bell, the Duke of Rutland; Jean Dawnay, Prince George Galitzine; Alla, Dior's house model, married film director Robert Capa. Others entered the fashion business. Dorian Leigh set up the first Paris based model agency in 1959 and the impeccably dressed Jennifer Hocking joined *Harpers & Queen* as fashion editor. When marriage was not in the offing, a film contract often was. Capucine, house model for Fath and Givenchy, starred in numerous films including Blake Edwards' *The Pink Panther* in 1963 and Clive Donner's *What's New Pussy Cat?* in 1965. Suzy Parker played a cameo role of an existentialist turned model, and Dovima played the character of Marion in the 1957 musical comedy *Funny Face*. Parker continued her acting career appearing in a handful of films, most famously alongside Joan Crawford in *The Best of Everything*. Top models of the day could earn up to £2000 a week in New York; Barbara Goalen, the 'guinea an hour girl', was Britain's highest earner. Suzy Parker, Revlon's first face and Sunny Harnett, the Clairol girl, made thousands for exclusive contract work. When Christy Turlington met Dovima working in a diner in New York in the late 1980's, she told Turlington: 'Keep everything. I have nothing.'

The cult of beauty produced its own dramas. Models resorted to plastic surgery. Lude, a Russian model suffered an operation to reduce her breast size and trim her thighs. The surgery was primitive, Lude was never again able to wear low cut dresses because her nipples pointed upwards. Competition also provoked rivalry. Bettina Ballard in her memoirs recalls some of the catfights which would brew up during collection time: 'Sometimes there were terrific dramas such as Suzy Parker burning Fiona Campbell-Walter with a cigarette when Horst discovered Fiona's Nefertiti beauty and preferred it to Suzy's redheaded Texan beauty.'

Pierre Cardin with his line up of models at Orly airport in 1963. Cardin made the beautiful Japanese model Hiroko Matsumoto (second left) the star of the cabine

Audrey Hepburn was the ultimate ambassador of Givenchy elegance, he dressed her on and off the screen. In *Breakfast At Tiffanys* Hepburn's gamine image inspired a new ideal of woman

Modelling was fashionable. Society girls flocked to the agencies, there was plenty of work. In the 1950s, fashion shows were an event on society's calendar: 'I had a lovely time modelling in Harvey Nichols every lunch and tea time,' said Zandra Fisher a young British model, 'They let me choose the clothes I wanted to wear and I used to doll myself up to the nines to float around. Mummy brought all her friends in for tea. It was very sociable.'

Numerous 'how to' books and a spate of autobiographies were published during the decade all of which helped raise the profile of the profession. Jean Dawnay, the former air hostess turned model, writes a typical rags to riches fairy tale story in her 1956 autobiography *Model Girl*. 'I was having more publicity than was good for me and getting rather bored with tag, "she has just returned from Christian Dior," even the local butcher had a picture of me stuck beside the carcasses and on Saturday mornings as I stood in the meat queue, he would bellow in a loud voice: "Make way for the pin up girl." But make no mistake about it being glamorous. Every day is hard work and modelling far from being a world of fantasy is one of harsh facts.'

► END

The Pop Aristocracy

The haute couture madam of the Fifties with her dignified pose, twin set and pearls was overthrown by the ingenue of the sixties. The new model had pinprick breasts, gawky limbs and the space saucer eyes of a girl who had just discovered sex. She was photographed with her long skinny legs through wide angle lens, on the streets as the girl about town, in mini skirts, see through shirts, in kinky boots and hipster trousers. Every woman wanted to look like her, and every man wanted to sleep with her, the model girl became the **It Girl** – a pin up symbol of the sexually awakened Sixties.

It was the explosive youth culture of Britain which fostered the new model image: the Britain of The Beatles, The Rolling Stones, Mary Quant, a nation which was made up of Colin MacInnes' 'Absolute Beginners'. Fashion was no longer about class, breeding or the haute couture salon; it was born on the street, in jazz bars – Mary Quant mini skirts, Tuffin and Foale tailoring, Vidal Sassoon five point haircuts, and a new dress for every Saturday night – the stifled couture world of tea time manners and Louis gilt chairs, society models and gentleman photographers was turned on its head. The new models came from the suburbs and the photographers from two-up-two-downs in the East End.
'I had a choice at this time, aged sixteen, time Monday, 4:30 in the afternoon. I could either be a jazz musician, an actor, or a car thief...They – from Mars or wherever they are – said I wouldn't be a fashion photographer because I didn't have my head in a cloud of pink chiffon. They forgot one thing. I love to look at all women,' said David Bailey in his book of portraits *Box Of Pin Ups*.

Photographers David Bailey, Terence Donovan and Brian Duffy, the Terrible Trio, as they became known, defined the look of the decade. Armed with their lightweight 35mm cameras, bags of cheek and bravado, The Terrible Trio, stripped away the artifice of fashion and introduced spontaneity and sex: 'Before, fashion photography was posh, it was Beaton doing royal stuff and fashion plates. It was silent.' said Bailey's former assistant, the photographer John Swanell, to *The Independent* 'Then Bailey brought it down to basics and everyone was turning the music up. Photographers did want to lay girls and drive flash cars.'

It became standard practice for The Terrible Trio to have relationships with their models, and the intimacy produced the era's most potent images. Bailey and Shrimpton became the couple of the decade, a symbol of the Sixties alongside The Beatles and Mary Quant. Between 1961 and 1964, **Jean Shrimpton** was Bailey's favourite model, her rise to fame meteoric. A convent girl raised in the backwaters of county town England, she graduated from Lucie Clayton, found herself working with Brian Duffy for an advertising job where she was spotted and snapped up by raffish David Bailey. From there, Bailey and Shrimpton embarked on a tempestuous three and a half year relationship, during which time they shot *the* fashion images of the early decade.

Bailey used Shrimpton's ambiguous appeal, making her a symbol of breakaway youth. Shrimpton's poses were free of the grandeur of her predecessors. She posed for Bailey wearing evening gowns but seated on the floor, in tailored suits but with her knees hugged to her chest, or running through the streets as the young girl about town. The look of innocence proved irresistible. By 1961, the two were working for British *Vogue's* new 'Young Idea' pages, by 1962 they were summoned to America: 'England has arrived,' said Diana Vreeland when they walked through the Conde Nast office. After splitting with Bailey, she continued to model and remained in the public eye with boyfriend, the actor Terence Stamp. By 1964 she was famous enough to write her memoirs. She retired young: 'I know how lucky I was to arrive on the scene just at that time.'

Jean Shrimpton

Above, Actor Terence Stamp, the star of Alfie at the premier evening party for the play, with partner Jean Shrimpton in 1964

Right, Celia Hammond, who graduated from modelling school with Shrimpton in 1960. By 1961 she was on contract to Queen magazine making her name as the sex kitten

Celia Hammond

OUS
ES RECORDS
E MODE
ATTUS :
1 MODELES
968
DE 75 A 175F

Nicole de la la Margé

1,50 F. GDE-BRETAGNE : 3,6 SH | SUISSE 1,60 FR. S - U.S.A. 45 CTS - 11 JANVIER 1968

Shrimpton and Bailey were at the centre of a youthquake which ran havoc through fashion. Everyone was doing something. Designers Mary Quant, Marion Foale and Sally Tuffin, Ossie Clark launched their democratic, modern ready-to-wear; the boutique Quorum opened in the Kings Road and became the hang out in London. There were jazz clubs, cappuccino bars, new cinemas, and art galleries – the stuffy atmosphere of the city was blown away. Media opened up to the voice of youth. On TV, Cathy McGowan, the presenter of pop show *Ready, Steady Go* became a fashion icon in her own right; in print, society magazine *Queen* was overhauled to reflect the new spirit and *Vogue* gave birth to its Young Idea. And in 1965, youth found its most radical expression yet in the fashion magazine, *Nova*. Everyone wanted to be a part of the scene, London models had never had it so good.

In the Sixties, models were watched as closely as film stars in the Forties. Shrimpton, Elsa Schiaparelli's granddaughter **Marisa Berenson**, **Celia Hammond**, Norman Parkinson's protege, the blond sex kitten **Jill Kennington**, **Tania Mallet**, **Sue Murray** a later Bailey girl, dominated fashion, they set trends. Modelling had none of the professional trappings it developed later, models did their own hair and make up and provided the hosiery, shoes and accessories for a shoot: 'It was fun everyone knew each other,' says London model agent Peter Lumley, 'the best models were middle class or suburban girls with no inhibitions. The London girls were popular not only because of their look, but because of their outlook.'

Models were the centre of attention; they were the mascots of the pop generation. Celia Hammond had an affair with guitarist Jeff Beck, George Harrison married **Patti Boyd**, Mick Jagger had a fling with Chrissie Shrimpton, Jean's younger sister – the fantasies that filled the pages were lived day in, day out. 'Everyone had affairs with everyone, photographers with models, photographers with fashion editors, models with rock stars – it was the done thing,' says Caroline Baker, then fashion editor of *Nova*.

Patti Boyd

Psychedelic colours flashed through fashion imagery in the late 1960s

Left, French model Nicole de la Margé, the visual image of French Elle. She appeared on over 150 covers in as many guises

Shrimpton and Hammond paved the way for the face of the Sixties: Twiggy. Born Leslie Hornby in 1949, daughter of a working class family from Neasden, Twiggy became the darling of the decade, six and half stone and aged 16. With her flat chest, Bambi eyes, gawky limbs and Ariel presence, Twiggy took the sex object image one stage further – she was pre-adolescent. Her boyfriend/manager Justin de Villeneuve, **Mary Quant** and Vidal Sassoon created Twiggy. Quant made her the mini skirt, Sassoon the geometric fivepoint haircut, Villeneuve the Pierrot eyes and the promotion. Twiggy was a phenomena of the Sixties, a wide eyed stick thin ingenue with an adorable Cockney accent. She was as different from the sophisticate Suzy Parker of the Fifties, as her lookalike Kate Moss was to become to the sex goddess image of Cindy Crawford in the Nineties.

Above, Twiggy and Justin de Villeneuve; the gold sports car was a gift from Toyota

Left, Twiggy in the woodlands - photograph by Jeanloup Sieff for British Vogue

Below, Twiggy made her debut in the Daily Express, as 'The Face Of '66....the Cockney kid with the face to launch a thousand shapes.'

Twiggy was the first model of international celebrity.

On her arrival in New York she was mobbed, like The Beatles and The Stones before her, she made the cover of *Time* magazine, and was the subject of a television documentary by the photographer Bert Stern. Asked in interview about her figure Twiggy replied: 'It's not really what you call a "figger" is it ?' For three years Twiggy *was* fashion; her hairstyle, make up, clothes were copied worldwide. She licensed her name to ranges of make up, hosiery, garments and plastic dolls as manufacturers competed for the spin-off of her fame. She retired at 19 to be welcomed back in 1971 as Twiggy the actress, the lead in Ken Russell's film *The Boyfriend*.

The fashion revolution was not exclusive to London. In Paris, Courrèges, Paco Rabanne and Yves Saint Laurent like **Quant** were making a business out of designing fab shocking gear for the young. Fashion shows changed as dramatically as the fashion page. When Courrèges presented his **Space Age collection** in 1965, his models did not simply show the clothes, they became Space Age, dancing in experimental kinetic movements to *musique concrete* in white knee high boots, visors and plastic mini skirts. Courrèges took his experiment seriously.

'The model girls are tall crew-cut amazons' wrote Alison Adburgham fashion editor of *The Guardian* in 1965, '...with splendid sun-tanned limbs but flattened chests. In the dead white salon they create an impression of sterility. And yet, that is not exactly it. Nor was the spectator exactly right who spoke of it as a collection for lesbians. Nearer right, was the one who said that it suggested *un troisième sexe.*'

Designers were out to shock; wholesome and pretty did not make headlines. Quant turned her shows into a groovy party; **Paco Rabanne** turned his salon into a vibe room, where his exotic models stoned on marujana swayed to electronic music in chainmail dresses, bare feet and *bindi* spots. Shock built on shock. In America, Rudi Gernreich designed his topless bathing suit and presented it on his favourite model **Peggy Moffitt** and made the headlines worldwide. In Paris, Yves Saint Laurent revealed breasts on the catwalk in see-through shirts. Bald heads, pregnant models, even identical twins – all appeared as the hunger for novelty became increasingly contrived.

'I want model girls who look like real people to wear my clothes which are for real people. I want girls who exaggerate the realness of themselves not their haughty unrealness like couture models do.' Quant launching her plastic footwear in 1967

Courrèges, Paco Rabanne, Yves Saint Laurent and

Quant made a business out of designing fab

shocking gear for the young

Above, Angular bodies and geometric garments: Spanish designer Paco Rabanne
made his celebrated chainmail clothes with pliers instead of needle and thread

Left, Naomi Sims – one of the first black stars. In 1969 she was on the cover of
Life magazine, she said 'Being black and female should be considered an asset.'

Above, The moon landing beamed Space Age fantasies into fashion, models projected the illusion of weightlessness. Vogue April 1967

The pre-pubescent child woman, embodied by Twiggy, toppled the chic sophisticate from her perch. Modelling Courrèges bikinis in 1968.

In the dead

Above, Unzipped: Linda Keith models an Ossie Clark design of 1966

Centre, Models expressed modernity in graphic bodyshapes. Dress by Mary Quant

Right, Peggy Moffitt, Rudi Gernreich's swimsuit model caused uproar going topless

white
salon they create an impression of
sterility

The new model pose, seated cross-legged on the floor, 1965

Jean Shrimpton, for Carita hair salons, 1965

German-born model Veruschka (opposite) who saw herself more as an artist than a model, starred in Antonioni's movie all about the world of fashion, Blow Up

GRAN PREMIO INTERNAZIONALE DEL FESTIVAL DI CANNES 19

METRO-GOLDWYN-MAYER PRESENTA UNA PRODUZIONE **CARLO PONT**

UN FILM
DIRETTO DA **MICHELANGELO ANTONION**

BLOW-UP

VANESSA **REDGRAVE** DAVID **HEMMINGS** SARAH **MILE**

A new breed of art photographer

A new breed of art photographer began to develop a very different model image. Whereas Shrimpton and Twiggy had set the blueprint for hundreds of lookalikes, the new models were chosen for their eccentricities and uniqueness. **Veruschka**, who made her name as the star of *Blow Up*, was one of the first 'extraordinary' models. Born Countess Von Lehndorff, the art student daughter of a blue blooded family of Prussian descent, Veruschka saw herself more as an artist than a fashion model. She contrived her own bizarre image; an animal-like prowl, a heavily exaggerated East European accent and an all black wardrobe. Veruschka was exceptional, she even suggested fashion stories to the editors of magazines; photographers found her an intriguing subject: 'I thought it would make a more interesting photograph if I change the colour of my skin, giving the image a strangeness that would distract attention from the often very boring dresses,' wrote Veruschka in her 1986 book *Trans-Figurations*, 'as a model I could transform myself into many different characters. Soon I began to paint myself as different animals and plants, knowing that they are more beautiful than we are.' Veruschka helped art direct her own shoots, transforming her own image as she thought fit. Her artistic modelling was fully realised in *Trans-Figurations*, shot by her then boyfriend, Holger Trulzsch. In a series of stunning *trompe l'oeil* photographs, Veruschka meticulously painted her own nude body to the colour and texture of the natural background. From appearing as the artificial painted fashion model, Veruschka was literally camouflaging herself into nature.

The 1966 movie *Blow Up*,

The 1966 movie *Blow Up,* directed by Michelangelo Antonioni, opened the can on the sex drugs and rock and roll behind Swinging London, sending up the folly and vanity of the fashion ego. It starred David Hemmings as sex mad photographer Thomas (a character allegedly based on David Bailey) and the model Veruschka as the ultimate sex object. It was an artful satire on Swinging London. David Hemmings treats his camera as a penis extension and his profession as licence to screw his way round fashion's beautiful people. Whereas Hollywood's *Funny Face* had characterised the typical fashion photographer as the debonair Fred Astaire who has an affair with Audrey Hepburn, in *Blow Up*, Hemmings plays the fashion photographer as God. 'All of a sudden it seemed that every adolescent shutter bug with a masturbatory imagination had converged on New York with a light meter in one eye and dollar signs in the other,' wrote *New York Magazine*.

By the mid Sixties,

By the mid Sixties, top model fees were in the thousands, and top league photographers, Avedon, Bailey, Bert Stern, Helmut Newton, William Klein were pulling in mega bucks. **Stern**, a photographer who was both art director and fashion snapper made more money than any before. His showcase studio in East 63rd Street was a vertical production line of studio, editing room and graphic design studio and a pleasure dome of library, dining room, basketball court and sound stage. If a model wanted to be anyone she had to be round Stern's uptown and Andy Warhol's Factory, downtown.

Battlefield chic by Hans Feurer for Nova 1971

In the heat of mid decade, the euphoric bubble burst. The clean cut optimism of the early years started to wane. Space Age dreams made way for Hippie idealism: mini skirts dropped to maxi lengths, there was no longer a place for the wide eyed It Girl as fashion started to question and shock. It was the dark and druggy Biba image which was aspired to, not the go ahead kid of Quant. The 1966 movie *Blow Up* provided the bang.

The second shock was the publication of a new fashion magazine, *Nova*. It set out to provoke, to upset the status quo, which it did consistently for some eleven years. *Nova* was the first women's fashion magazine to address the emerging issues of female liberation: orgasm, contraception, childbirth, and men were all written about frankly and illustrated by hard hitting images. The approach to fashion was equally provocative. Molly Parkin, a former art student, was the first fashion editor followed by Caroline Baker, who worked from 1967 until the demise of the title in 1975: '*Nova* fashion was really an art director's trip, a gallery,' says Baker, 'Helmut Newton might come in with an idea for a shoot with a girl in a whorehouse covered in mirrors, or Guy Bourdin with an image of a white room with a girl with plaster in her hair...the photographers vision came first. It had nothing to do with fashion trends.'

Nova was a storming success. It realised that women wanted more than cookery cards and knitting patterns, that women had a sense of humour and that they wanted to be treated intelligently: 'I have taken the pill. I have hoisted my skirts to my thighs, dropped them to my ankles, rebelled at university, abused the American Embassy, lived with two men, married one, earned my keep, kept my identity and, frankly...I'm lost.' (read the coverlines of *Nova* Sept 1968). Photography was always at the cutting edge; during the Vietnam protest, Nova ran a fashion shoot on combat gear shot by Hans Feurer; Baker devised a fur coat shoot which was modelled by down and out women; photographer Bob Richardson shot a story around the 'suicide' of model Anjelica Houston. No subject was taboo. It gave space to the photographers who were to dominate fashion through the early years of the Seventies: Helmut Newton, Guy Bourdin, Bob Richardson, Hans Feurer, and *Nova's* own art director/photographer Harry Peccinotti all shot regularly for the magazine. 'Ideas' as opposed to clothes always came first. The approach, pioneered by *Nova*, was later shared by French *Vogue* and in America, by *Harper's Bazaar*; a sign that women everywhere wanted something more than pretty girls in pretty clothes.

Brian Duffy shot 'How to undress in front of your husband' with Amanda Lear, for *Nova* in 1971

English model Penelope Tree was another exotic. Five foot ten, incredibly lanky, Tree was not a conventional beauty. But on camera, her tragic face and shy manner evoked the weird and wild spirit of the late Sixties. Bailey first shot Tree for *Vogue* when she was seventeen, she later moved into his all black house in Primrose Hill, but it was in America that Tree came into her own. Alexander Liberman, art director of US *Vogue* described Tree as 'a curious, sort of non-fashion young woman.' Richard Avedon befriended Tree and turned her into the spirit of the times. Avedon shot a legendary series of black and whites of her for American *Vogue* in 1967. Tree wearing a beatnik black trouser suit, black stockinged feet; her impish face under a heavy fringe appears in a frieze of images in which expressions run from shielded, to anger, to joy to disillusion. 'The Sixties was a decade of great hope and deep misgivings,' said Liberman, '...and I think Avedon caught all this in this picture.'

The model who had 'come alive' in the early Sixties, now looked in every sense real. Working relationships became intense. In 1967 photographer Bob Richardson shot a 16 page series for French *Vogue* featuring his favourite model, Donna Mitchell, which broke the boundaries of fashion shoots. Mitchell plays a character in an erotic narrative set on a Greek island, she remembered it as: 'One of the greatest times I ever had. It was for real. They thought we were really odd, but they didn't care. I played blackjack with the guys, they were singing and bouzoukis playing – then suddenly it became serious – all the men started dancing with me and smashing glasses. It got completely out of hand,' said Mitchell, 'The place was a wreck, I was drunk out of my fucking mind.'

Left, 'The Heavenly Suited' by Caroline Baker for Nova, 1972

Right, Penelope Tree photographed by Just Jaeckin for Vogue, 1968

Above, Romantic escape: summer dressing for Nova, 1972

Left, Donna Mitchell in Greece by Bob Richardson, French Vogue, 1967

no one
wanted their models to look
professional
or polished

Eric Clapton and Alice Ormsby-Gore on their engagement in 1969

Richardson was pushing the fashion image towards a documentary style realism, his images were brooding, sometimes disturbing. 'At their most intense his photographs reflect the search of a man who aimed "to climb inside the model" – to look for their soul,' writes Martin Harrison in his history of fashion photography *Appearances*. In later years, Richardson explored the theme of drug culture in ever more poignant and beautiful images.

As the clouds over Vietnam started to thicken, and seedy political scandals started to erupt, the fashion image became increasingly expressive and passionate. Ingenues were replaced by moody sultry figures, brightness for darkness, the clothes seemed a minor point. 'Fashion photography in the 1970s,' writes Harrison, 'no longer incorruptible, would follow the lead of photographers such as Helmut Newton and Bob Richardson.'
And the model, no longer innocent, would follow suit.

Designer Ossie Clark, who had lived every bit of the Sixties, ended the decade presenting collections on his houseboat which was moored on the River Thames. Like the photographers of the day, Clark blurred the divisions between reality and fashion. Guests sat on Turkish carpets strewn on the floor, mothers breast fed their babies, Amanda Lear, Patti Boyd modelled, slinking barefoot, stopping to share a joint now and then and chat.

From Hip Glamour

The beautiful people of the post-hippie era exhuded glamour, models as well as designers and photographers became celebrities in their own right

pie to

Above, Christie Brinkley: California glamour girl, one of the highest paid models of the decade, she even produced her own pin-up calendar

Left, Ossie Clark (3rd left) and party guests Edina Ronay, Patti Boyd, Peter Sehlinger, Eric Bowen embracing Bianca Jagger, kneeling, Manolo Blahnik

The Seventies was a decade of extremes, a decade of upheaval: women fought for their rights, racial minorities fought for their rights, campaigners pitched on Greenham Common and unemployment hit an all time low. In such a climate, all fashion could do was keep on moving. The model image hurtled between tweedy ladies, karmic hippie chicks, outdoor girls and disco dolly birds. The 1970s model was a woman in search of an identity.

In the early years of the decade, the fashion image experienced a dramatic turnaround. A new group of photographers emerged who were given unprecedented freedom to explore their fantasies. Sex, and its many connotations, became a central issue. The model was no longer a pretty girl showing the latest hemline and handbag; she cross-dressed, played *ménage à trois*, faked orgasms and acted in scenes of lesbian lust. Sexual identity was explored in every which way.

A handful of fashion magazines: *Nova* in England, *Twen* in Germany, American *Vogue* under Diana Vreeland and French *Vogue* led the way. Some of the most daring and provocative images were created during these experimental years. Photographers were given carte blanche and it was they who defined the look of the model. Instead of Mary Quant Girls or Dior Ladies, there were Helmut Newton sirens, Sarah Moon dolls and Guy Bourdin's oval faced waifs. Names and personalities were irrelevant, even fashion trends, all was in service of the photographer's art.

Berlin born photographer, **Helmut Newton** was the greatest influence over the decade. Newton's images were a potent mix of sex, wealth, violence and power. Through his lens the sexual libertine of the 1960s, metamorphosed into a dominitrix. There had always been a strong sexual undercurrent to Newton's work in a career that stretched back some fifteen years, but it was the libertarian atmosphere of Paris in the Seventies which allowed him to explore the depths of his obsession. It was here that his pictures of a 'world without men' made him a star.

In Newton's meticulously crafted photographs, tall leggy blondes, indistinguishable from one another, strolled in furs and diamonds, their bodies glistened with oil, limbs taut as steel, in one pure vision of sexual power. He liked groups. Models, posed in two and threes, whipped up lesbian frisson, or gyrated on steel turbines and writhed on columns against industrial backgrounds.

Over the years, Newton gathered a group of models with whom he worked regularly. He preferred flawless blondes and strong featured dark haired women. A Dutch model Willie Van Roy, actress Charlotte Rampling, Lisa Taylor, Jerry Hall were long-time favourites. 'What is interesting in a woman who is totally clothed by fashion is to see something one shouldn't see,' said Newton in *Frames from the Edge,* a documentary film about his work, 'I am only interested in the external features – how can I photograph the soul?'

Newton's spin with perversity proved controversial. Feminists believed Newton's images were degrading to womankind. They made their protest heard. One fourteen page long fashion shoot entitled 'The Story of Ohhh...' which was published in US *Vogue* (May 1975) really stirred the wrath. The story featured the sultry blonde model Lisa Taylor who plays the part of a sex starved madam. One image of Taylor, legs apart and looking predatory while a man passes in the foreground, caused most upset: 'The fact that her legs were open didn't seem very important to me,' Newton once explained, 'She had that big skirt on. But it caused scandal. People cancelled their subscriptions.'

Sarah Moon's photographs were disquieting beneath the feminine, nostalgic façade, Vogue 1976

Each photographer developed a type

Fantasy seeped into fashion at every layer

Fashion's caravan went on tour and discovered ethnic beauty. Clive Arrowsmith, Vogue 1976

of woman

Newton was not alone. He was one, most provocative, of a group of photographers who reflected contemporary mores in fashion imagery. A French photographer, **Guy Bourdin**, was another groundbreaker. Bourdin's work featured in French *Vogue* through the early years of the Seventies, Joan Juliet Buck, now editor of the title, worked as a stylist for Bourdin: 'In terms of the magazine, it was about photographers expressing themselves which really had more to do with aesthetics and less to do with trends,' says Buck. His contribution was to give the fashion story a narrative which gave 'meaning' to the model image. Bourdin explored a romantic and vulnerable image of women. His models, describes Buck, were typically waif thin with round oval faces disguised in kabuki make-up. They appeared love lorn creatures, adrift from the world.

Right, The glamour girls shone in the late Seventies under the ring flash, Vogue 1979

Below, A beauty frieze: from Bath-house, the controversial series from Deborah Turbeville, Vogue 1975

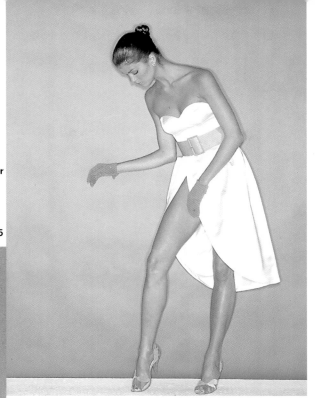

The female photographers of the era were just as controversial.

Former fashion editor, Deborah Turbeville, whose work appeared in English and American *Vogue*, explored the link between beauty and alienation. Her images were made to be read rather than merely ogled, yet the clear meaning was elusive. Turbeville chose models with an unusual beauty and through them was able to suggest the complexities of self image. Her images were startling because they expressed none of the showiness or happiness normally associated with fashion image; in atmosphere they were claustrophobic, even depressing. The *Bath-house* series of 1975 which fired one of fashion's longest running debates, discussed in *Women In Fashion*, was thought particularly disturbing, even immoral. The story, ostensibly a swimsuit shoot, features a group of models in the setting of a Turkish steam room but interpretations stretched to gas chamber victims and drugged out glamour girls. Evading the enquiry, Turbeville later explained that she simply wanted to compose a picture around a group of women.

The fashion shoot turned into an elaborate affair.

Photographers spent days, even weeks, creating fashion stories. The preparation was meticulous and the relationship between model, photographer and editor, intense. Through this process, Bourdin, Newton and Turbeville changed the focus of the fashion image by giving a weight of meaning beyond the mere description of clothes. Commercial clients picked up on the trend. Guy Bourdin produced a series of high concept campaigns for the French shoe designer, Charles Jourdan and the designer Madame Grès. Sarah Moon, who frequently worked with the model Susan Moncur, provided the heady opiated images for the successful label, Biba; Deborah Turbeville's advertising work included cosmetic and underwear catalogues. The reaction to one advertisement by Turbeville for Xavier's hair salon in New York in 1975 was recorded by Diana Vreeland in her photographic anthology *Allure*: 'Now this is new – doesn't this picture look exactly like a brothel.'

The era of experiment came to an abrupt end in the mid Seventies. The magazines were simply not selling in sufficient quantities. In a series of dramatic shakeouts, Diana Vreeland was deposed from American *Vogue* and *Nova* closed down in 1975: 'It was the end of a remarkable period,' says Caroline Baker, 'one which will never be repeated.'

Fashion needed a new face, a new direction, which spoke directly to women. The new wind came from America: 'While the look in Paris became more decadent – tiny tear stained red heads photographed by Guy Bourdin looking dead, or immense Teuton torturers photographed by Newton looking dangerous – the US reverted to its natural obsessive concern about health and diet' wrote Joan Juliet Buck in *Vogue*, 'Exercise, fresh air sport and bran and molasses, the mucus free diet, the vegetable diet and Biele total health occupied American girls while English girls were still putting Biba Brown on their cheeks.'

A new school of models broke who exuded health, vitality and natural beauty. The first to come through was **Lauren Hutton** – a rangy blonde with a crooked nose and a gap between her front teeth. As fashion started to yearn for a less dressy image, Hutton's flaws, a disaster for a model in years previous, became lucrative attributes. Born and raised in the Florida swamps, she was more interested in the great outdoors than in fashion. It was by chance that Hutton ended up modelling. She left her home town, with the mission of reaching Africa, when she found herself in New York without money or a bed to sleep in. Hutton began work as a bunny in a Playboy Club, and later became a house model for Christian Dior earning a meagre $50 a week. Consistently model agencies turned her down; Hutton's image was considered too kooky. The break came when she took a job as a fittings model for a *Vogue* shoot. Diana Vreeland spotted her and packed her off to see photographer Richard Avedon. He alledgedly described Hutton as 'Just another Florida type on waterskis,' but started to work with Hutton, teaching her the poses of Twiggy, Veruschka, and Penelope Tree and eventually turning her into a Hutton brand of model, once describing her as 'the link between the dream and the drugstore.'

Hutton hit the cover of *Vogue* in 1966 but it was another eight years before her natural look really came into its own by which time she was signed to Ford models. She made history in 1973, when cosmetic giant Revlon, in search of a fresh image, signed her as a contract face for a record $400,000. It was the largest sum ever paid to a model and the start of what was to become a multi-million pound business in image models. Hutton was the liberated woman through and through. She refused to wear tight underwear and bras on shoots and even helped direct her image: 'They used to drip me with diamonds. I mean two million dollars worth of rocks at every session and I just kept saying: "This is not the way to go.." they promised they wouldn't be chandeliering me anymore...then it became nothing but gold chains. Solid gold chains all the time!' Over the years her image evolved. She would disappear for months to travel: 'I would lose track of civilisation for months at a time, never look in a mirror and when I came back my face would have changed. My smile could be real again and I would look different.'

Hutton's transformations proved compelling in their own right. Women identified with Hutton, she became a household name. Back in 1971 she joked that she would be selling granny cosmetics in the year 2000, and in 1995 Hutton made a return on the catwalk of Calvin Klein.

Right, A ring of English roses in Laura Ashley's campaign

Left, Natural woman Lauren Hutton

Youth – all smiles, health and coquettish charm invaded fashion in the mid Seventies led by the American outdoor girl

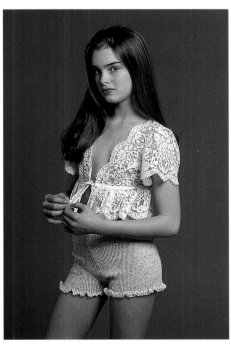

Fashion's love of innocence liked girls at an early age. Model/actress Brooke Shields as she appeared in the film Pretty Baby

Once Hutton proved that a more natural femininity appealed to women, a slew of sexy, wholesome types followed. Blond beach babe **Cheryl Tiegs**, sexy **Christie Brinkley**, freckle faced **Patti Hansen**, discovered working on a hotdog stand, and the late **Margaux Hemingway**, daughter of Ernest followed. In a fashion industry notoriously dictatorial, these models, true to their images, began to exert a small degree of autonomy: 'I never lost that extra ten pounds that makes people look emaciated...and would never let anyone pluck my eyebrows,' said Hemingway to *Vogue*.

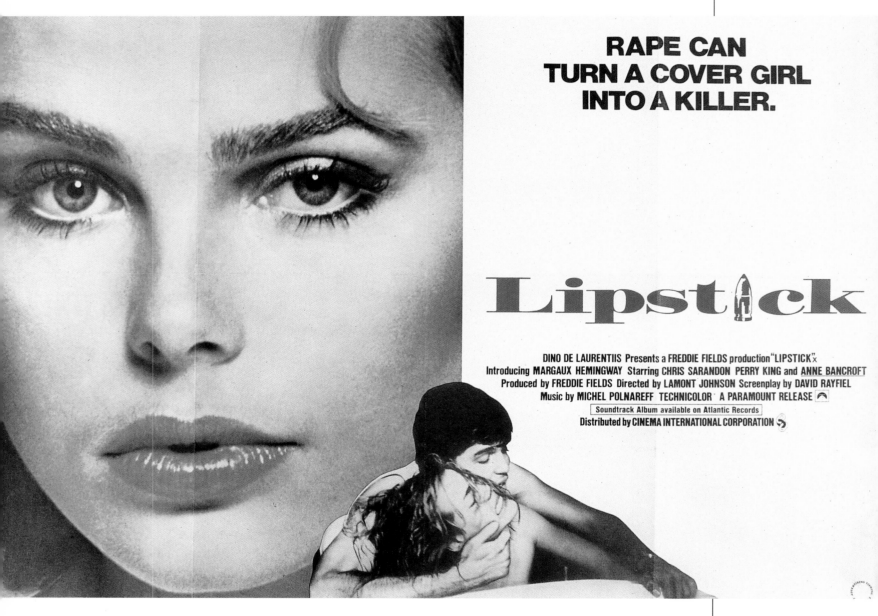

RAPE CAN TURN A COVER GIRL INTO A KILLER.

Lipstick

DINO DE LAURENTIIS Presents a FREDDIE FIELDS production "LIPSTICK" x
Introducing MARGAUX HEMINGWAY Starring CHRIS SARANDON PERRY KING and ANNE BANCROFT
Produced by FREDDIE FIELDS Directed by LAMONT JOHNSON Screenplay by DAVID RAYFIEL
Music by MICHEL POLNAREFF TECHNICOLOR A PARAMOUNT RELEASE
Soundtrack Album available on Atlantic Records
Distributed by CINEMA INTERNATIONAL CORPORATION

The American models started to dominate fashion. The clean shiny glamour girl became the new ideal. And nowhere was it clearer than in advertising. American cosmetic companies launched global campaigns and international brand models, and fees hit an all time high. Cover Girl cosmetics signed Cheryl Tiegs for a staggering $1.5 million, Fabergé paid Margaux Hemingway $3 million. The exposure allowed leading names to launch other careers. Tiegs sold her name to a line of designer denim and bikinis, Lauren Hutton and Margaux Hemingway moved into films; Hutton appeared in several films that included *Paper Lion*, *The Gambler* and *American Gigolo,* while Hemingway landed the star role in the pulp thriller *Lipstick*.

Far Left, Margaux
Hemingway star of the
pulp thriller Lipstick,
one of a spate of fashion
films released including
The Eyes of Laura Mars
and Calendar Girls

Centre, Cheryl Tiegs'
designer denim
Left, Freckle faced wild
child Patti Hansen

Fashion imagery changed with the clean ideal, again the lead coming from America. Photographers **Duane Michals**, **Arthur Elgort** and **Alex Chatelain** led the new school. Dreamy fantasy gave way to dynamic action as magazines drew fashion closer to reality. Models exuded life and energy. They danced, swam, 'worked in offices' and stretched on sunlit beaches. The model pose changed from the lean Sixties line to great striding shapes made by supple exercised limbs. Francesco Scavullo, who gave *Cosmopolitan* its sexy image, was known for the 'strut', Richard Avedon for figures which leapt off the page and Arthur Elgort for dancing girls. Suddenly the pages smiled as fashion loosened up.

Working woman by Duane Michals for American Vogue, 1976

The imagery of fashion and the industry change dramatically

Left, American designer Halston epitomised glamour

Below, Yves Saint Laurent in 1975, hero of the modern woman

Paris was slower to pick up the image of modern women but it did eventually when the *pret à porter* revolution got under way. Designers realised that the business of *haute couture*, reliant on women with money, was beginning to look sadly outdated. Values had changed. Cheap chic clothes were needed for the market place and a different mode of presentation. This was the beginning of the modern catwalk. Although *pret à porter* design had existed for some years, the collections had always been undersold in terms of shows. That all changed when the Japanese designer **Kenzo**, behind the hugely successful Jungle Jap label, launched in Paris in the early Seventies. He turned it into a spectacle.

Kenzo extended the catwalk into a stage, for an audience almost four times the size of a traditional salon show. And instead of a neat line up, he asked his models to improvise. **Marie Helvin**, a Kenzo favourite, describes in her autobiography *Catwalk* a particular show that was entitled 'Cover Girls': 'The girls went wild, clowning and somersaulting, doing the rhumba and dancing cancan, showering each other with feather-like confetti, waving sparklers and baring their breasts like the girls on Rue St.Denis... sophisticated Paris had never seen anything like it before...they roared. After Kenzo there were no hard and fast rules about catwalking, there were fads. First the wild look, next the dancey phase, then a patch with vampy solos half way down the runway.'

Right, Grace Jones on the catwalk, 1976

Below, Bianca Jagger at Studio 54

Studio 54

The *pret à porter* catwalk shows grew in size and stature. In Milan there was Gianni Versace, Armani, Missoni and Valentino; in Paris, Sonia Rykiel and Dorothee Bis, Thierry Mugler, Claude Montana amongst many others and in New York, Calvin Klein, Halston and Bill Blass. And two models – **Jerry Hall** and **Pat Cleveland** – emerged as catwalk queens. They introduced fun and sex to the staid catwalk; designers and the audience adored them. It was not entirely their own idea. The catalyst was a hugely talented fashion illustrator, **Antonio Lopez**. His charismatic personality made him the centre of fashion in Paris. Lopez' circle included Newton, Bourdin and the young Karl Lagerfeld.

Pat Cleveland, a former fashion student, was a protégé of Lopez. She met him in New York, relates Michael Gross in *Model*, following him to Paris where she found herself in the limelight. Cleveland, one of the first black models to break through to the top, was a one woman show. She could dance like no other. Each season she was a new character, one year Dorothy Lamour, next Josephine Baker, and she was out every night with Lopez, being seen.

Jerry Hall, a six foot blond from Texas, became Cleveland's double act. Hall, who was discovered on a St Tropez beach wearing a tiny pink crocheted bikini, met Lopez on arrival in Paris. And it was through him that she began to make her mark. The story goes that Lopez introduced her to Helmut Newton. He first shot Hall for a porno chic shoot for *Photo* magazine, and then for the cover of French *Vogue*. The image of Hall biting a man's cheek set the ball rolling. Her fame spread, soon everyone wanted her: 'I started living with Antonio and two other guys and we were going out every night and our friends were drag queens and transvestites. They taught me how to do my make up, I was hanging out with Grace Jones and Pat Cleveland,' said Hall. The double act grew into a power act, and Cleveland and Hall were swept into the rock and roll world. Hall was booked for the cover of Roxy Music's album *Siren* and ended up dating Brian Ferry and later Mick Jagger.

During the late Seventies the glamour life was epitomised by the drug-fuelled disco world of Andy Warhol's New York club, Studio 54. It was here that the era's models found their second home. Any model who wanted to be anyone hung out at Studio 54, playing to the paparazzi to catch her own 15 minutes of fame. The world's top models Hall, Cleveland, Patti Hansen, Marisa Berenson, Elsa Peretti were some of the many that passed through the doors with fashion's brightest stars.

Jerry Hall and Pat Cleveland, the catwalk queens, for Chloe, 1979

Marisa Berenson

Berenson in Hanae Mori eveningwear, Paris 1972

Fashion in the Seventies also had an appetite for the exotic. Ethnic beauties broke through the ranks, the most famous of the period was the beautiful Somalian born **Iman**. Her life story was even changed to suit tastes. Iman Mohamed Abdulmajid was, so the story went, discovered as a tribeswoman in Kenya. She was, in fact, the wealthy daughter of a diplomat. Iman went on to to become one of the highest paid models ever. She was reputedly paid $100,000 for a catwalk show in Munich; compared to the going rate of $1500 a show, the fee was astronomical. Hawaiian/American **Marie Helvin**, a Bailey protégé and later his wife, became a household name. She featured so regularly on the pages of British *Vogue*, that readers apparently wrote to complain. Pat Cleveland was the first black catwalk model of note, and in 1974 **Beverly Johnson** became the first black cover girl of American *Vogue*. They opened the gates for a generation of black models.

Above, Marie Helvin for Ossie Clark, 1977

Right, Beverly Johnson, the first black model to appear on the cover of American Vogue, 1974

Ethnic beauties came into fashion, the most famous of the period being the exotic Somalian beauty, Iman

Vivienne Westwood in August 1977

The artifice and the high camp of the glamour years was finally thrown off by **Punk** which exploded onto the streets of London in 1976. Youth rebelled against authority and rejected the material world. Punks evolved a style of offensive fashion, the intention was to **shock.** From its birthplace in Vivienne Westwood's and Malcolm Mclaren's **Sex shop** at the bottom of the Kings Road, revolt spread. The image of femininity which had led fashion through the century was ripped to shreds. The model would **never be the same** again

► END

Heroin

of

The grand splendour of 1980's fashion was epitomized by Chanel haute couture, and sent up by Jean-Paul Gaultier

es
the day

Punk unleashed the energy of the street and made London the centre of fashion. During the early years of the decade, a group of radical designers emerged. Their credo was individualism and anarchy; their role models, not Belgravia ladies, but the twilight inhabitants of clubland. London rewrote the rules of fashion; there was no canon of beauty, or uniform to follow, the emphasis was on personal expression.

Clubland gave birth to the scene: 'Like carnival, the clubs of the early 1980's – Billy's, Taboo and Blitz – occurred regularly but not every day. They permitted contained (sartorial) unruliness, which was often not tolerated on the street where such costume would sometimes arouse verbal abuse or even physical violence,' writes Minna Thornton in *Women in Fashion*, 'A plenitude of styles prevailed, excessive and heterogeneous. Both the social and sexual order was reversed and mocked. For a night men could be women, the unemployed could dress as kings and queens, as Hollywood stars, aristocratic Regency fops or ecclesiastics.'

From these clubs, a cult of style for style's sake emerged which expressed itself in what became known as The New Romantic movement. Designers, pop musicians and film makers including Boy George, Spandau Ballet, the film maker, John Maybury, the performance artist, Leigh Bowery and designers Body Map and Stephen Linard were at the centre, and all fed one from the other.

It was a period of great entrepreneurship and great vanity. Clubgoers dressed up to be seen, and photographed. The more provocative and witty the outfit the better. There were no rules. And it was not long before the carnival atmosphere spilled out on the catwalk. When it did, there was uproar. Young design duo, Stevie Stewart and David Holah, behind the label, Body Map, were true iconoclasts: 'Body Map's shows were just sensational. For the first time, there were big women on the catwalk and old, young, male and female – non professionals. One year the singer Helen Terry modelled ....the atmosphere was fantastic, it made you want to leave your chair and dance,' says Caryn Franklin, ex-fashion editor of *i-D* magazine. 'It was all about the individual; designers were really reflecting club and street culture and they found their models on the street, in clubs or amongst friends. I remember going to the Paris collections and thinking is that all the models are going to do? just walk up and down? Of course, that was the norm.'

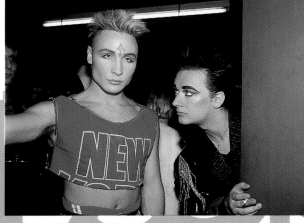

Boy George (right) and Marylin: Fashion icons for their generation

The only that existed were those rules to be

'Vogueing' a dance based on catwalk posing; started in the black gay community of New York, it swept dancefloors when Madonna raised the underground style to public level with 'Vogue'

sm
broken

During these hedonistic years, the influence of the street was taken to its extreme. **Vivienne Westwood**, the designer who created punk fashion, achieved the unimaginable. She fused the rebellious style of the street with tribal and historical costume and created street cults on the fashion catwalk. Her collections attracted a fanatical following. Every season, the models adopted a different guise, and with that guise came a different set of poses and gestures. 1981 was the year of swashbuckling Pirates (which was shown in the Club for Heroes), in 1982/3 Buffalo: 'The giant thing about my clothes – the way they make you feel grand and strong – is to do with the sexy way they emphasise your body and make you aware of it,' said Westwood of the whirling and gamboling models who came tumbling down the catwalk during the Buffalo collection. 'My clothes look tribal and therefore, they communicate signs themselves.'

The London guard demolished the idea of fashion

uniform and gradually eroded the notion of an ideal woman. 'Outrageously bizarre street fashion is a phenomena peculiar to London. It occurs in other major cities but on a much subdued scale, and the original ideas are often rooted in the London scene,' writes fashion critic Sally Brampton, then of *The Observer*, in *The Fashion Year* (1983) 'It is an advantage born of out disadvantages – the class system, poverty, lack of education and unemployment. The English are an eccentrically creative breed who, when they find no established focus for expression, explode violently into unconventional style, music and fashion.'

Above, Vivienne Westwood and muse Sara Stockbridge pick up Designer of the Year award at the Royal Albert Hall, 1991
Top, The Witches Collection by Vivienne Westwood, autumn/winter 1993/94

Marie Sezneck, Christian Lacroix's favourite model

Designer John Galliano was a slightly later recruit. His presentations were pure fantasy. It was clear from Galliano's very first show (his 1984 graduate collection from Central St Martins) how different his approach would be. The collection entitled 'Les Incroyables' immediately convinced the audience of Galliano's genius. His models appeared as though resurrected from the French Revolution, drifting barefoot, eyes whitened with pale mascara, in tattered clothes sprinkled with cobwebs and dust. Every season, a different set of characters emerged: Napleonic heroines, Anastasia on the run, Blanche Dubois, and shipwrecked Victorian ladies. The shows were almost hypnotic and the characters compelling. They seemed to touch on a fantasy of escape which was innately female. In the 1986 Galliano collection called 'Fallen Angels', a Botticelli beauty, pregnant and barefoot appeared on the catwalk in a sodden voile gown, her make up streaked, her hair bedraggled: 'I didn't do the watersoaked muslin to shock anyone. It was just beautiful to see a woman walking down the catwalk and wearing this dress, and to see the flesh move behind this film of gauze,' said Galliano.

John Galliano's fantasy presentations have grown more and more elaborate and wonderful. Christy Turlington for Galliano's summer collection, 1994

London's fertile counter culture was given a second home on the pages of a new wave of style magazines: *The Face*, *i-D* and the short lived *Blitz*. Each title quickly developed its own distinct fashion image. Terry Jones, formerly the art director of *Vogue*, reversed the mode of the glossies, all high artifice and perfection, and introduced street fashion photography onto the pages of *i-D*. Real people were photographed in their own clothes: 'There was never a directive, we simply went to clubs, went out on to the streets and found interesting people who looked good,' says Caryn Franklin, 'It was fashion in its rawest form – glossy, unmarketed and full of ideas. '

On the pages of *Blitz*, the fashion images were highly stylised and directly reflected the DIY dress which had emerged through clubland. At *The Face*, publisher Nick Logan, the former editor of *NME*, made the vital tie between England's music and fashion cultures. Fashion imagery, which became increasingly statement led, was there to be read, not merely ogled. The style magazines were mould-breakers and became a breeding ground for the country's foremost talents in graphics, photography, music and proved an excellent casting couch for alternative models.

Deconstructing the fashion image
by Mark Le Bon for i-D, 1986

The Japanese **vision** of woman as intellectual, sober and asexual, wa's the **antithesis** of the Western sexy chic ideal

The female image made strange: Comme des Garçons autumn/winter 1983/84

Although London in the early Eighties gave fashion a new cast and a new meaning in a very vital and expressive form, the ruptures were not exclusive to the city. Even Paris, the bourgeois stronghold of fashion, was under threat. **Jean-Paul Gaultier**, a designer heavily influenced by London's club and street scene, broke through the ranks of the establishment. Like Body Map and Westwood, Gaultier projected a street-led, multi-ethnic vision of fashion. His designs were madcap parodies of contemporary culture, and his choice of models reflected that. Transvestites, half cast models, models with piercings and tattoos all appeared in his extravagant shows.

The gloss lip sexpot model took her final blow when a group of avant garde Japanese designers, led by Rei Kawakubo of **Comme des Garçons**, launched in Paris in the early Eighties. The Japanese rejected the bourgeois notion of clothing as seduction, and designed not to prettify, but to provoke ideas. In doing so they deconstructed the image of femininity.

Comme des Garçons' first show terrified the Paris fashion establishment. Lights flickered on and off, models wearing unstructured strategically torn loose black layers catwalked to a cacophony of discordant music, but the most shocking aspect of the presentation was the model image. The girls were not pretty: stringy locks of hair were greased back, their faces smeared with charcoal make-up, lips left bare and eyes heavily ringed in black: 'C'est Hiroshima...sans amour,' thundered one French journalist. Never before had a fashion show caused such upset; Rei Kawakubo was even accused of degrading the female image: 'Creation is the expression of mood, of anger, of hope' says Kawakubo, 'So although each piece of clothing is important, the collection has a further huge significance in expressing what I want to say... the models are just one part of a whole.' Fellow Japanese designer, **Yohji Yamamoto**, was equally uncompromising. Yamamoto's shielded breasts and hips under black unstructured shrouds; the attributes which throughout time have provided the focus of design. The total image was distant and asexual. But by presenting the model as part of a concept, the Japanese were able to question. One point was made clear: woman did not need long hair, big breasts and a fecund figure to prove herself feminine.

The knock-on effect of the avant garde in London and Paris was to provide an alternative type of model. As the influence filtered through, magazines started to incorporate increasingly diverse faces and body shapes. Short haired androgynous models, naidic creatures, characterful individuals, ethereal soulful figures all appeared on the pages. Readers were experiencing variety and that was the point, the model had become a blank canvas through which to reflect ideas.

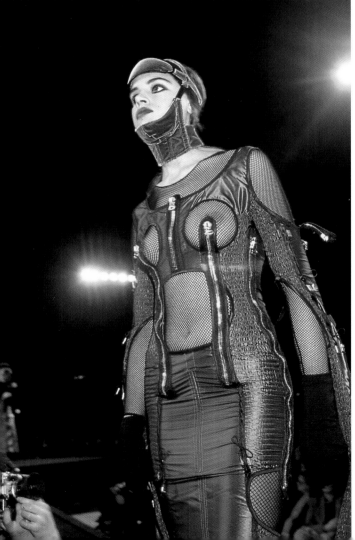

Far Left, Issey Miyake autumn/winter 1989/90

Left, The body fetishised at Jean-Paul Gaultier autumn/winter 1989/90

There was an inevitable backlash. In the mid

Eighties, orthodox designers reared up and launched the supersexy Amazonian model: she was all body rather than all concept. The new model, typified by the impossibly perfect **Christie Brinkley**, was ten pounds heavier than her Seventies counterpart, her breasts (often silicon) were pneumatic, and her body the new aerobicised figure. She launched to lure a new generation of career women into the fashion fold and she was the perfect foil: sexy and powerful.

Designers pushed the ideal to its extreme in a Darwinian

fight to create the perfect female. The lead was taken by Tunisian born designer, **Azzedine Alaïa**. His designs, painstakingly tailored from stretch fabrics, eulogised the female form. And models fought to be in his shows; being an Alaïa girl meant you owned one of the best bodies in the business. Alaïa's favourite, also his muse and confidante, was Farida, a *jolie laide* corkscrew haired Algerian model, closely followed by a young Naomi Campbell. His shows attracted a cult like following. Grace Jones, a diehard fan, Anouk Aimée and Carole Bouquet, came back season after season to watch Alaïa's homage to the body beautiful.

Fashion's love of the female figure turned into an

obsession by the mid Eighties. Designers wrapped and swathed the body in clinging Lycra micro clothes photographers cropped heads out of the picture, filling the frame with impossibly perfect figures. The obsession reached such a degree, Gaultier was able to parody the trend in the conical bra dress which was designed for Madonna's 'Who's That Girl' tour. Fashion even named its own icon in the shape of **Elle MacPherson**, a 6 ft tall Amazonian model who simply became known as 'The Body.'

Sex, power and status became the bywords of Eighties

fashion. In 1986, British *Elle* launched, taking the hip, successful woman as ideal. Power by day meant the executive striding through crowds, document wallet in hand, and power by night meant the vamp, clad in fetish black leather and corsets. By the mid Eighties, the sexpot model, along with her shoulder pads, dominated the fashion page: 'The fashion model said energy, dynamism, there was little personality it was all about the clothes, the power shoulders' says Lucinda Chambers fashion director of *Vogue*.

Everything got bigger in the Eighties. Fashion

was fashionable; the elite sport blossomed into a global consumer industry. Designers licensed their names into perfume, accessories, chocolate, cosmetics – brand names became so lucrative Yves Saint Laurent was able to float his business on the stock market. Fashion entered every facet of life. Nothing was quite as grand or indeed pretentious as the biannual *pret à porter* collections; broadcast through satellite and TV stations world-wide, the collections turned into a media spectacular. In 1986, the Paris shows were attended by 1875 journalists and around 150 photographers: nearly a four-fold increase on the figures recorded for 1976. Front rows were studded with celebrities, backstage awash with champagne.

Azzedine Alaïa spring/summer 1986

Right, Iman for Thierry Mugler autumn/winter 1986/87

Far Right, Career girls go: Vogue, July 1987

French designer, Thierry Mugler, was the master showman. His presentations were of Cecil B. de Mille proportions. Accompanied by dazzling light displays and epic soundtracks, Mugler's models appeared on six inch high stilettos, bodies articulated by rhinestone corsets like siren figures from a sci-fi novel. By 1984, Mugler's shows had become such an event he was able to stage a grand spectacular attended by 4,000 paying public. 'Religion had hit Mugler,' wrote Jackie Moore, fashion editor of *The Glasgow Herald* 'He presented us with golden winged angels in purple satin, the Angel Gabriel in pleated gold lame and finally a Madonna descending from the roof and looking suspiciously like model Pat Cleveland.'

Fashion shows became increasingly fantastic, designers were out to woo the cameras. Fellow French designer, **Claude Montana**, sent out battalions of alien models in clouds of B-movie dry ice. Ostentation was not confined to Paris. In Milan, Versace dressed troupes of sex divas who showed more body than dress, Valentino cloned his models as swanky film star heroines, Giorgio Armani was so repelled by the artifice, he temporarily abandoned live models for static presentations. In New York, designers opted for elite presentations. Major photographic models Roseanne Vela, Christie Brinkley and Iman guaranteed maximum camera appeal.

The eighties were wealthy and acquiring. The French industry tapped into new money's demand for old money habits and revived the business of haute couture. **Karl Lagerfeld** was made head of Chanel in 1983, and the first new couture house for thirty years headed up by young designer Christian Lacroix was launched in 1987 with a £5million investment. The resurrection of *haute couture* brought about a revival of the old style muse figure. Designers recruited contract models to project the house image to the world. Karl Lagerfeld's choice for Chanel was a lithe dark haired aristocrat, Inès de la Fressange. The muse contract was exclusive. When de la Fressange accepted the title of Miss France, she was swiftly deposed from the house in a wave of public scandal and was later to be replaced by the Bardotesque Claudia Schiffer. **Christian Lacroix**, chose older model Marie Sezneck. Yves Saint Laurent, the darling of the jet set crowd, worked with the elegant black model, Moonia and Loulou de la Falaise. The pure social prestige of the model hit an all time high during these buoyant years.

Cosmetics houses and advertisers adopted a similar approach. International brand Estée Lauder signed Paulina Porizkova, a flawless chiselled featured ice queen for an estimated $6 million over ten years. Donna Karan created her own career woman ideal in the model Rosemary McGrotha, who appeared in TV and print campaigns throughout the late 1980s.

Above, Inès de la Fressange at Chanel couture, spring/summer 1983
Below, Esteé Lauder's contract model Paulina Porizkova

Left, A striking pose: Claude Montana
Opposite, Pat Cleveland as the Angel Gabriel for Mugler's gala show 1984

The booming advertising industry led the model into every facet of life. Blown up larger than life on billboards, beamed through TV screens, the glamour models sold coffee, cars and calculators. Everywhere one looked, she was there; lips wetted, hair glossed ,skin glowing. Women aspired to be her – not merely to buy the clothes from her back. The image of the model was so prevalent it turned up in the poorest backwater of Harlem in a highly stylised dance called Vogueing which was invented by the most marginalised group of society – the gay black transvestite community. The dance which was based on the poses and gestures of the high fashion model swept through the clubs of New York. The phenomena was made subject of a documentary film *Paris Burning* in 1987 and catapulted onto the world-wide pop platform when Madonna swooped in on the trend and released 'Vogue.'

Photography pushed the high style of the Eighties to its extremes. In America, designers issued bumper lifestyle catalogues. The most influential and one of the most successful was a series of campaigns which photographer **Bruce Weber** completed for Ralph Lauren. The images which reeled out in a fictional story over the decade were a eulogy to the America of pioneers and heroes. Weber shot the same cast of models, (such were the budgets that Weber was able to live with his models) over and over again, transforming them into characters.

Kirsten Owen by Nick Knight for Yohji Yamamoto

Nick Knight for Yohji Yamamoto, 1989, art direction by Marc Ascoli

As the romance and glamour of fashion became more pronounced over the decade, likewise the avant garde became increasingly artful. Comme des Garçons brought out a magazine called *666* which featured highly creative conceptual shoots which worked way beyond the hard sell of clothes. Photographers Peter Lindbergh and Hans Feurer, and the artist Cindy Sherman were some of the select few commissioned. Yohji Yamamoto had highly stylised catalogues, several photographed by Nick Knight, a British photographer who had emerged from the early days of *i-D* and one of the most innovative photographers othe day. Knights' highly stylised and sublimely beautiful images remain an acute reflection of the Eighties as a decade of hedonism and artifice.

► END

To be super, a model had to become more than just a paper face, she needed what the fashion industry called the X-factor

Super mod

Model product: introducing Naomi Campbell, Claudia Schiffer, Karen Mulder – the doll size versions. Private Eye takes a different angle, 1996

The face of the modelling was changed when Linda

Evangelista flippantly remarked 'We have this expression, Christy and I: We don't wake up for less than $10,000 a day.' The first models were hired from the ranks of seamstresses, Charles Worth, the forefather of the design industry paid wages on a par with a floorsweeper, their reputation was sluttish. Over one hundred years later model had turned supermodel earning more in a year than most would earn in a lifetime, with a celebrity that exceeded rock stars and Hollywood icons, and a power which commanded their own terms of work. Fame, fortune, power and beauty – the super-models were desired on every count. Every man wanted to sleep with her, every woman wanted to be her, and every girl wanted to grow up to be her. Supermodels were famous for being beautiful, they were the ultimate dream of self made success.

Supermodels were the creation of the designer decade – a decade obsessed by image, by power

and by glamour. Previous eras had model stars – Twiggy, Barbara Goalen, Jerry Hall – but none matched the fame or the fortune of a supermodel. Claudia Schiffer, Naomi Campbell, Linda Evangelista, Cindy Crawford and Christy Turlington became the idols of an era. Never before had so many people become aware of the fashion model. They were a phenomenon.

To be super, a model had to be more than a paper face, she needed what the fashion industry called the X factor: 'She has 10,000 expressions and has a real love story with the camera. She is unquestionably beautiful but more than this, she emits qualities that make her one of the most beautiful models in the world,' once said Karl Lagerfeld of his one-time muse Claudia Schiffer. The term supermodel was first coined in the late Eighties, just as recession hit. The fashion industry like every other consumer industry fell into hard times. But it was the supermodels with their remarkable mix of power, beauty and fighting spirit who kept the glamour dream rolling through those bankrupt years. But what fashion could never have predicted is quite how popular these girls would become.

But the supermodels had all the ingredients. They were a compendium of beauty for the Nineties with that all important expression of character: 'From Christy Turlington's stupendous pout to Tatjana Patitz's sleepy feline eyes, Linda Evangelista's boyish crop to Cindy Crawford's much debated beauty spot, or Naomi Campbell's Puckish grin, they're emphatically individual,' writes Sarah Mower when British *Vogue* introduced the supermodels on the legendary cover of 1990. Between them every type of beauty was covered. Turlington was a Nefertiti beauty – timeless, Schiffer and Campbell both child woman, Crawford, the perfect American dream girl, and sharp featured Evangelista, the super boy woman.

Claudia Schiffer and Cindy Crawford were the two most impossibly perfect supermodels. Schiffer, discovered at a Dusseldorf discotheque in her teens, was a true Bardotesque beauty. She was everyman's fantasy, blond, curvaceous with a hint of vulnerability, and rocketed to fame when photographer Ellen Von Unwerth spotted her and cast her as the Guess Jeans girl. When Karl Lagerfeld made Schiffer the face of Chanel her fortunes were made. By 1991, Schiffer was worth around $12 million.
'The most famous woman in the world. . .' once said designer Paco Rabanne, 'and what is she, a coathanger!'
Cindy Crawford, born Cynthia Ann Crawford the daughter of an electrician father and bank teller mother from Debalk Illinois, was about to become a chemical engineer when her modelling career shot into the stratosphere. Hard work and solid professionalism turned Crawford, a knockout beauty, into the all American dream girl. 'Women identify with me,' said Crawford in British *Vogue*, 'Perhaps they look at me and feel that I am strong and make money and I don't have to be a man to do it. I'm not playing a man's game in the sense of neutralising myself. Modelling is one of the only women's jobs where you don't have to play down your femininity.' She was the ultimate model and the ultimate career woman. Her career shifted into super mould after she appeared in *Playboy* 1988. Suddenly Crawford reached a whole new male audience. By 1991 Crawford had appeared on over 300 magazine covers, she held contracts with Pepsi and Revlon and presented her own fashion show, MTV's *House of Style*.

Cindy Crawford

Right, Dreamgirl Cindy Crawford for Donna Karan

Centre, Yasmeen Ghauri for Valentino

Far Right, Christy Turlington for Jil Sander

Yasmeen
Ghauri

Christy
Turlington

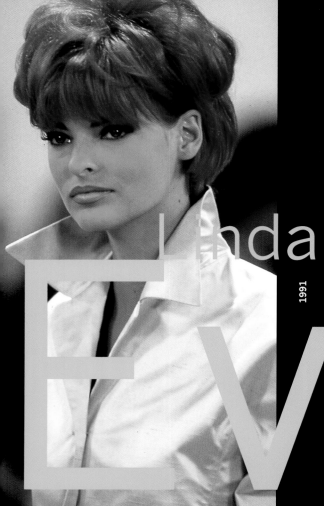

1989

1995

1991

1996

Linda

Evang

1994

1994

elista

Genetically the models were perfect, professionally they were outstanding. But they did not make it alone. Fashion photographer **Steven Meisel** was catalyst behind Evangelista, Campbell and Turlington. He was the superlative model meister and supreme fashion photographer. On a reputed $2 million contract to American *Vogue* Meisel became the fashion world's image dictator. Where Meisel and his crew went, fashion followed. Steven Meisel, who was born to a middle class family in the New York borough of Queens, apparently devoted most of his life to model watching. In his early years, Meisel devoured women's magazines; by his teen years he was blagging his way into shoots, his coup was a glimpse of Twiggy, and doorstepping Richard Avedon's studio. By the time he took up his first fashion job as an illustrator for the trade paper *Women's Wear Daily*, he knew everything there was to know about modelling and photographic style. He trained his models to suit, teaching them the expressions and body language.

Meisel worked with **Christy Turlington**, a half Salvadorian daughter of an air pilot and air hostess from Walnut Creek, California. Turlington's career was already firmly founded; she was signed to Calvin Klein on a three year $1.2 million contract working with photographer Bruce Weber. Turlington severed her contract with Klein and chopped off her hair in 1989, reputedly fed up of being an exclusive image girl. But she had proved so successful, Klein reinstated the deal allowing her to take up other work.

Linda Evangelista was the next recruit. By the time she met Meisel in 1986, Evangelista was already a pro. From a middle class Canadian family, Evangelista started her modelling career as a shop girl earning $8 a hour. After being spotted at a Miss Teen Niagara beauty pageant, she worked her way to Paris. Like Meisel she turned herself into the ultimate composite. She studied every model pose in the book and knew fashion inside out: 'She has a tremendous desire for success... she is no more or no less beautiful than many other woman, but she wants it really bad,' allegedly said Gerald Marie her husband and head of Elite model agency.

Photographer **Peter Lindbergh** cast Linda regularly in the mid Eighties, but it was Meisel who turned her into a chameleon. She first hit the headlines when she chopped off her hair in 1988, long hair being in at the time. At every turn she reinvented herself, a hair colour, a hair cut, a different set of poses. When Evangelista appeared on the catwalk in 1994 with hair dyed a shade of tomato red, the hip had their hair dyed to match. And well past the model sell-by date of 24, she stayed at the top of the tree into her late twenties and beyond. Evangelista rewrote the rules of modelling.

The ultimate chameleon: the many faces of Linda Evangelista, from 1989-1996

Turlington introduced the young gauche Naomi Campbell to Meisel. Campbell, a dance student from the Italia Conti stage school, born and raised in South London, was disarmingly beautiful. The first black cover girl of French *Vogue*, she was also Alaïa's model star and had appeared on the cover of society magazine *Tatler* shot by Michael Roberts before moving to New York in 1989. Meisel, antenna always on the alert for new stars, took Campbell under his wing. In her first shoot for US *Vogue*, Campbell proved her model mettle posing as a boy with sideburns, one of many transformations. When Meisel shot Evangelista, Campbell and Turlington together in a raunchy lingerie shot and dubbed them The Trinity, soon every magazine and designer followed suit; the three together were an almighty power.

The supermodel phenomena exploded like a fireball. Beauty and skill were only part of their success. Just as their collective beauty formed a new ideal from icons past, so too did their profession. The supermodels were an enigma. They combined the role of the unofficial models of the Twenties, the wealth of the society women, and the celebrity of film and pop stars. As their fame grew, fees escalated and celebrity blossomed. The supermodels had to be seen:
'There was a strategy that had to do with getting noticed as something more than a model – it was simply a question of publicity of getting her to the right parties and openings,' Meisel reputedly said of Campbell.

The supermodels were the first professional models to break out of fashion. Within a space of two years the public were au fait with their names, faces and earnings, lovers and lifestyles. They were afforded the fame that only Hollywood stars had achieved before them. The springboard to fame was George Michael's 'Freedom 90' video in which the new school of star models appeared en masse. Suddenly a completely new audience of MTV viewers were introduced to fashion's star models. *Les top du top du top models*, as French *Vogue* called them. And fame allowed the models to sidestep into other careers. They were courted by the media, by film and TV moguls who quickly caught onto the fact that the supermodels were public hot property. Cindy Crawford became anchor woman to the MTV fashion series *House of Style*, Campbell, recorded a record (which flopped) and dabbled in film taking a cameo role in Spike Lee's film *Girl 6*. And a slew of product launches followed. Schiffer issued calendars and an exercise video, there were supermodel Barbie dolls, and even a theme restaurant, The Fashion Café in New York which opened in a blaze of media hype in 1995.

As fame grew, fees grew. Until the supermodel arrived, the wealth and power in fashion had lain in the hands of the client and the designer, and there was one flat rate for every model. In the Eighties, the supermodels took power into their own hands. Fashion was turned on its head. Catwalk fees escalated to £30,000 for a 30 minute showing, in 1970 models did their own hair and were paid £50 a show, Turlington's Calvin Klein contract topped $3 million, Schiffer grossed around $12 million. They travelled in limousines, wearing dark glasses. Bodyguards protected them, assistants opened fan mail, accountants invested their earnings, publicists protected their image, consultants advised their careers. They even had their own cartoon which appeared weekly in *Private Eye*.

Fetish fantasy, at Versace

Naomi Campbell

Supermodels guaranteed instant publicity for designers.

Versace was the first to realise this when he started to book them *en masse* in the early nineties. For their appearances during the Milan collections they were reputedly paid nearly £30,000 each. Under Versace's signature blue lighting, trooping down a disco square catwalk, these very beautiful women really were a fantastical vision. Chanel followed suit. Soon every designer was bartering for their patronage, and winning their smiles meant feting the supermodels, bowing to their every whim and demand.
'I like them but I hate the stardom created around them,' said Valentino to the *Sunday Times* in 1991, 'They should walk, show, change, walk show again. That is what I ask them, not to be stars but to become Valentino Women.' The epidemic spread. Up until the late Eighties show reports had consisted of straight critiques of the cut and cloth; names were never mentioned. By the turn of the decade, it was Linda's phantom pregnancy, Naomi's tantrums and the food on the supermodels' plates which made fashion news. The clothes were almost incidental.

In true celeb style there were supermodel affairs. Where

Jerry Hall was made famous for her relationships with Bryan Ferry and Mick Jagger, in the Eighties the pattern was reversed, rock and film stars were the sidekicks of models. During Campbell's fling with Mike Tyson (who was already married) she appeared ringside and made front page headlines. 'She had a great body and she's scared of nothing,' allegedly said Tyson, 'that's why I like her.' The saga continued with Robert de Niro, Eric Clapton and a failed engagement with Adam Clayton. Evangelista, after her divorce from Gerald Marie, was tracked with Kyle Maclachlan. The world's paparazzi snapped Schiffer's marriage to magician David Copperfield and gobbled news of their divorce. But the icing on the cake was Cindy Crawford and Richard Gere. Rumours were building about Gere's supposed bisexuality, which apparently stirred such concern that the couple placed a full page £20,000 advertisement in *The Times*: 'We got married because we love each other...We are heterosexual and monogamous...Reports of a divorce are totally false...We both look forward to having a family.'

Supermodels dominated fashion into the early

Nineties. Never before had there been so much interest in fashion models. But an inevitable backlash was brewing. The first blow came in 1993, when designers started to complain of extortionate fees. The money issue was only one symptom of an industry that had become weary of diva attitudes: 'The myth of the supermodel was built on foundations where sex could be flattened and twisted into something we called beauty, and that beauty was twisted and starved into the image of a coat hanger. A coathanger from hell,' wrote the *Daily Mail*. The word supermodel suddenly started to taste sour. The Elite model agency severed dealings with Campbell, issuing the following statement: 'Please be informed that we do not wish to represent Naomi Campbell any longer. No amount of money or prestige could further justify the abuse that has been imposed on our staff and clients. All who experienced this will understand.' Supermodel bashing became the new media sport. By the mid Nineties, it seemed the model had lost touch with all reality. Supermodels were on their way out.

The supermodels dominated fashion into the early Nineties. Never before had the public taken so much interest in fashion models. But there was to be an almighty backlash

The springboard to fame: Vogue's January 1990 cover girls were shot by Peter Lindbergh. From left: Naomi Campbell, Linda Evangelista, Tatjana Patitz, Christy Turlington and Cindy Crawford

Back to Reality

There was a taste for normal looking girls with plenty of attitude. Carolyn Murphy and Jenny Shimizu were two of many

Kate Moss, a skinny nineteen year old from Croydon, with bowing legs and a minute five foot six frame burst into fashion in the early Nineties. Moss, the antithesis of the diva supermodels, looked sweet, streetwise and girly. Within two years, Moss had hooked a two million dollar contract for Calvin Klein and found herself pasted forty foot high, bare bum on show, on a Times Square hoarding. Moss, all attitude and no clothes, was fashion's new dream of reality.

'Reality' was to become the buzzword of the Nineties. On the catwalk, real fashion translated as minimal, urban clothes which had more in common with The Gap than haute couture and in fashion photography, as grainy documentary style shots of skinny suburban girls in whacked out poses. The healthy, sexy size 12 model was wiped from the face of fashion by an image of a dazed and confused youth. London broke the mould. From the point Moss emerged from *The Face* on to the international catwalks, there would be no one model look. Insouciance and individuality was what counted: 'It was all a laugh in the beginning,' says Moss 'I started modelling because there was nothing else to do in Croydon. It was an excuse to go up to London, I really liked working with the photographers – we would do a shoot, go on to a night club and take the nightbus home.'

Moss, with her dishevelled Sun-In blonde to mouse brown hair, streetwise poses and couldn't-care-less expressions, appeared the same self in front and out of the camera. The clothes she wore looked like her own. The illusion was her passport to fame. 'Of all the obscure objects of desire in Nineties pop culture, it's hard to think of one that inspires more attempts at analysis than Kate Moss, yet carries less clear meaning. The curious thing about Kate all these years on is that her waifish, untouchable, just-hard-enough-at-the-edges ordinariness that helped change the shape of the modelling business has now been installed as one of the Looks of our times,' writes Steve Daly in *The Face* (May 1996).

Moss and a group of extra-ordinary girls –
Rosemary Ferguson, who was reputedly discovered at a Tesco check out counter, Sarah Murray a lanky girl with strong features and a boyish frame – were propelled into fashion in the early Nineties by a group of London based photographers and stylists, collectively known as the 'dirty realists'. They revolutionised the fashion image in one of the most dramatic turns in over a decade: 'Fashion people used to look polished and pristine,' writes Marion Hume in *The Independent on Sunday*, 'They clinked when they walked with the weight of bold pieces of gold jewellery, and they had severe photogenic haircuts. But those dictating fashion now not only don't look smart, half the time they don't look washed. Most of all they don't look important.'

The dirty realist school was part of a greater cultural shift.
It represented a generation rebelling against the consumerism of the Eighties, trying to reclaim something of their own. It affected both fashion and music, and was the most vital expression youth culture had experienced for years. In America, there was a parallel movement in Grunge, a music stye that had emerged from the backwater of Seattle, and in chic France *la generation nulle*. It was British photographers, models and stylists, however, who gave a style to the movement: 'The fashion images of the new youth seem to lack any positivity save that of the junkie's gift for self delusion and bombed out apathy,' writes Michael Bracewell in *The Guardian*.

Moss, all attitude and no clothes, was fashion's new dream of reality

Right, Moss the waif for Calvin Klein, spring/summer 1993
Left, Kirsten McMenamy and Kate Moss for Marc Jacobs' 1993 Grunge
Collection for Perry Ellis

For the photographers involved there was a different agenda: to show youth as it really was. Photographer **Corinne Day**, a former model from Ickenham Kent, was a formative eye. 'I've always preferred to show people as they are. I love the style on the street in London, it's like no other place in the world. British youth has a sense of individuality and style unlike any other place in the world,' she said in interview for the *British Journal of Photography*. Her semi-documentary style was in stark contrast to the artifice and pomp of the Eighties fashion image. Models appeared as if she had stumbled across them in London bedsits; stringy unwashed hair, 'make up' – a mere stained lip and clog of mascara – they were photographed slumped on Draylon sofas, lying on ash-strewn carpets, leaning against stained radiator grills in ill fitting trousers and shrunk T-shirts. It was a raw vision, expressing a painful mix of grime and hope: 'When I was working with Corinne,' explains Kate Moss, 'she would always watch me off guard, off duty, lying on the sofa, hanging around, and these were the poses she asked me to replicate in front of the camera. Corinne thought I always looked better when I was pissed off.'

Day was not alone in her aims. Realism in its many variants was being swept into a fashion by a loosely connected band of photographers, each with an idiosyncratic style. **Nigel Shafran's** photographs expressed an exquisite sense of dislocation while **David Sims** focused on the character of his sitter, revealing their poses and gestures as if caught off guard: 'I used to shoot on the terrace of a studio, about fifteen foot of square surrounded by guttering. It became a bit of joke that I asked every body to scrape their nails in the dirt. We had an interest in making people look unkempt,' said Sims interviewed in *Dazed and Confused*. 'I wanted to inject a level of ordinariness into the fashion photograph.'

'I wanted to inject a level of ordinariness into the fashion photograph'

Punk couture: Guinevere Van Seenus by David Sims, Vogue, 1996

Realism spread, tipping out onto the catwalks of Europe. In Paris, a group of Belgian designers, collectively known as the Deconstructionists, were literally ripping apart clothes, letting the seams and innards of lining show through in the same way that photographers were bent on revealing the 'beauty' of unwashed hair and the blemished skin. Designer **Martin Margiela** pushed the anti-fashion trend to its surreal extreme. His 'designer' collections consisted of recycled and remade second hand clothing shown on a hotpotch of friends and *jolie laide* models in such lugubrious and boringly urban surroundings as subways and disused garages. **Ann Demeulemeester** preferred her models maudlin and tear-stained and sent them weaving through the crowd in tattered satin gowns, lipstick smudged, shoulders hunched. The new group made their shows as real as possible: models walked on ground level without posing or swinging their hips; even the designers kept a low profile: 'I think that if you are in the spotlight it can be a danger,' said Austrian designer **Helmut Lang** to *Harper's Bazaar*.

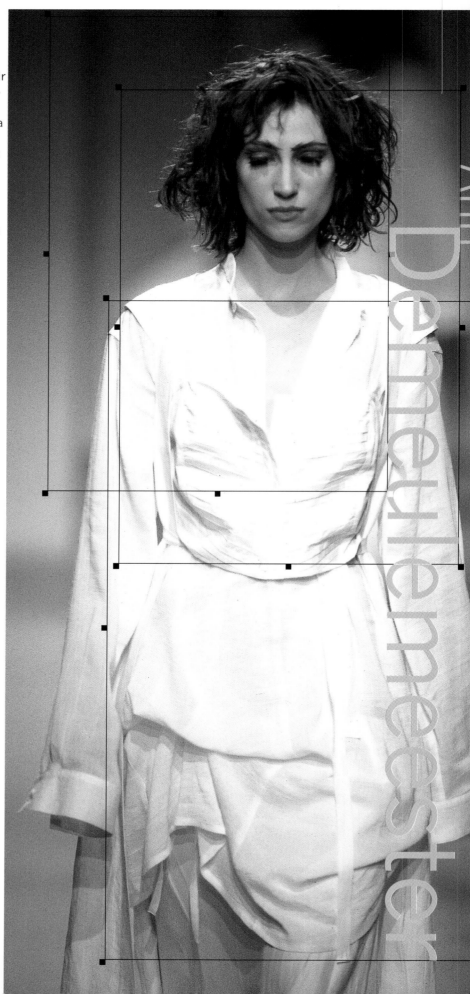

Right, On the catwalk for Demeulemeester's spring/summer collection 1994

Far Right, Filming Margiela's autumn/winter collection 1993/94

Martin Margiela

Reality came to a head in 1993 when the American fashion industry, desperate to tap the youth market, launched 'deluxe' grunge on the catwalk. London's dirty realists were shipped over-seas to redefine the American fashion image and with them came their favourite faces. London models had not been so popular since the heyday of the swinging Sixties. Day signed off the dole, and replaced Meisel for the prestigious campaign for Barney's New York department store; Sims went to *Harper's Bazaar*; the five foot six waif from Croydon, Kate Moss, snaffled the Calvin Klein campaign, a cover for *Harper's Bazaar*, and major runway shows: 'I'd never experienced anything like it,' says Moss, 'the fashion people in New York spoke their own language. I was petrified when I walked down the catwalk, I had only done a few shows before and I had to get dressed next to Linda Evangelista. Naomi took me under her wing, we were both from South London.'

The unimaginable happened. London's anti-fashion

idealists via the marketing whizzes of the American industry became the face of international fashion. They were cheaper and bleaker than the rest and expressed a priceless commodity of cool. The meteoric rise was unheard of in fashion's notoriously closed door industry. But the break was made, fashion no longer wanted perfection. A stampede of quirky individual models followed: the *jolie laide* **Kirsten McMenamy**, **Stella Tennant** an aristocratic punk with a slouchy pose and a ring through her nose, **Eve Salvail** a Canadian punk with a tatooed head and half Oriental **Jenny Shimizu**, a former motorcycle mechanic. '"Join us and become unique" is the paradoxical cry of an over the counter counterculture in which corporate advertisers get down, go underground and pass themselves as alternative,' writes Leslie Savan in *Alt. Culture*, a lexicon of contemporary cult style, 'Advertisers must tell consumers that they are each special individuals so that they will buy the same mass produced products – then consumers can construct their individuality by the unique combination of goods and services they buy.' Never before had fashion experienced such variety. Calvin Klein went as far as to cast an entire show with beautiful 'real' people, and real looking models for a CK show of 1994.

Funny faces: from left Eve Salvail backstage at Chanel, 1994; Kirsten McMenamy at Hussein Chalayan, 1996; old and beautiful for Issey Miyake, 1995

It did not last, for the general public fashion's stab at reality proved just too extraordinary. Grunge fashion flopped, the magazines lost sales, and the English crew packed their bags and were sent back home. Fashion then responded with the revival of glamour, and the passive waif was replaced by the sexual predator. Glamour's cheerleader was **Nadja Auermann**: a 6 foot platinum blonde with a staggering leg measurement of 45 inches. 'My legs were always unusually long, but I never thought of it as weird, just different,' she said to *The Face*. In 1994 Auermann scored a hat trick appearing on the covers of competitor magazines *Harper's Bazaar* and American *Vogue* as well as British *Vogue*.

Above, Amber Valletta for Gucci, spring/summer 1996

Left, Nadja Auermann for John Galliano, autumn/winter 1995/96

Right, John Galliano, spring/summer 1993

The revival of glamour

Above, Shalom Harlow for Yohji Yamamoto, autumn/winter 1995/96

Left, Where has the fantasy gone? Helena Christensen by Arthur Elgort, Vogue, 1990

As the waif was traded in, a new range of models emerged. They were diverse in looks but what they shared was an alluring mix of elegance and streetwise attitude. **Helena Christensen**, a Danish model with a curvy figure and pneumatic breasts, **Amber Valletta** a ginger haired beauty from Oklahoma and **Shalom Harlow**, an elegant dark haired, with a catwalk as slink as a jaguar moved from the peripheries of fashion into the main frame. And from the previous year's waifs and oddball models, only the true beauties survived. Kate Moss put on 5 pounds and reappeared with red lipstick, smoky eyes and a Veronica Lake hairdo in a sultry mode, Stella Tennant, nose ring removed, switched her slouching walk for an elegant stride.

The glam revival pushed the no hoper look out of fashion. It was the start of spate of revival trends which season on season sped from 1940s Hollywood sirens, to 1950s sweater girls, 1960s mods and IT girls and 1970s hippie chicks and glamour girls. Glossily packed nostalgia was the order of the day. As designers hurtled back through the history book of fashion, models swept through the museum of gestures from great models past. Lisa Fonssagrives' hand on hips elegance, Twiggy's knock knee poses, Lauren Hutton's swinging walk and the Cosmo Girl strut reappeared on the fashion page. Models who simply suited the period were hoisted from nowhere to become the one hit wonders of the season. Never before had there been such a rapid turnover of model faces and photographic styles. What remained from the early Nineties breakthrough and through all the pastiches of retro, was a strong sense of individuality and attitude.

On the wave of individuality came the next English model to make it big, a punky aristocrat by the name of Stella Tennant. From her leaving art school in Winchester in 1992 to becoming the contract face for Chanel in 1996, Tennant's rise to fame was meteroic. Her allure: quirky beauty, a tall angular skinny frame, a languid elegance and all important attitude was the antithesis to waif like passivity. Stella Tennant was the archetypal reluctant model, she scowled on the catwalk, her walk was all legs and arms, she wore a nose ring and she apparently talked back to designers which made her all the more irresistible. But her most important attribute was that she looked strange and new, she gave clothes an edge. Tennant risked being deposed like the rest of the wierd models but then she threw away the nose ring, learnt how to walk, and suddenly fashion considered her beautiful. 'Tennant is underneath a classic beauty,' says Lucinda Chambers, fashion director of British *Vogue*, 'porcelain skin, and fine angular features.' Of catwalking Tennant has said: 'you feel like a clotheshorse having its outside layer ripped off with a paint stripper and then reapplied several times a day.' When Tennant was signed as the contract face for Chanel, the worlds best known fashion house in 1996, the breed of individual models who started off as a novelty of the avant garde in the early Eighties was complete.

As the big business co-opted the individual, the style press promoted a new agenda and computer technology became the next muse of fashion. On the pages of *The Face* and *i-D* she/he, usually sexually ambiguous, was morphed, warped and contorted into a cyber figure and transfigured onto sets from a virtual world. Models' parts were collaged into hermaphrodites, natural eyes replaced by alien eyes and figures transported into hyper-real landscapes. In 1995, *The Face* voted the Quaintel paintbox, above any designer, the most influential force in fashion.

A group of photographers excelled in this virtual art. French photographer **David LaChapelle** created elaborately constructed worlds occupied by a cast of superreal human figures; **Andrea Giacobbe** used bizarre juxtapositions to communicate larger social issues while Dutch photographer, **Inez Von Lamsweerde**, used technology to turn her superficially glamourous images into surreal artforms. Perfectly airbrushed limbs protrude at odd angles, enlarged smiling heads are seamlessly morphed into skinny bodies in Von Lamsweerde's disturbing images.

Computer art had a parallel development in fashion. In the mid Nineties, a group of designers ignored retro to tackle the future. Shimmering plastic, industrial strength Tyvek paper, laser cut and heat bonded synthetic fabrics transformed the look and structure of clothes. Future fashion appeared on the catwalk when designers transported the virtual world to the fashion show. A Belgian designer, **Walter van Beirendonck**, turned the catwalk show into a virtual experience in 1995, when live models with surreal plastic-finish make up and robotic gestures were seen to interact in a virtual world of computer generated images.

The new model family by Andrea Giacobbe for *The Face*, July 1996

Right, Virtual catwalking: Walter van Beirendonck's W.&L.T. collection, 1997

In the 1990s, the model image appears in a multitude of guises. There is no longer a homogenous look or a universal ideal. Models have become as ephemeral as fashion trends, plucked up work for a few months and discarded. Girls with few photographs in their books are now appearing on the pages of quality glossies, a status which in the Eighties models would have had to work for years to attain. But the main thrust throughout the decade, and through techno revolutions and retro trends has been towards reality. It is perhaps fashion's grandest illusion. 'Supermodels still exist, evidently, but behaving like a diva and dressing like one – hitherto the *sine qua non* of being a super, is considered old fashioned and unsophisticated,' writes Lisa Armstrong, Fashion Features Director of *Vogue* (July 1996) 'The new girl's attitude is "Take me as you find me." And the fashion world does.'

Models no longer look or behave like models, the alphabet of gestures now runs from frowns to shrugging shoulders and on the catwalk from a dawdle to a stroll; every effort is made to blend in. At a 1996 catwalk show American designer Marc Jacobs pinned up the following sign in the dressing room:
'Boys and Girls
Please walk at a natural pace – not slow, not fast.
Please – no hands on hips.
No "turns."
No modelling!
Thank you – you are all beautiful, and we love you.'
As a further twist to the non-model trend, fashion is now reinventing the tradition of the first 'unofficial' models, at least in style. When in 1996 Chanel signed the punkish Stella Tennant, the granddaughter of the Duchess of Devonshire, as the face of Chanel, the turnaround from high glamour to individual eccentricity was made.

Through history the model has put on many guises. She has encountered scandal, prejudice, and has been rewarded fame and fortune and celebrity. She has become an icon of beauty for generations and has helped keep the fashion industry afloat. The model has a rich history. From faceless salon girl to woman of the world, to symbol of youth to supermodel and icon of beauty and back to seeming herself: 'I am just a model,' says Kate Moss. The modelling story has turned full circle.

The new face of Chanel 1996 – Stella Tennant

'Boys and Girls Please walk at a natural pace – not slow, not fast. Please no hands on hips No "turns". No modelling! Thank you – you are all beautiful, and we love you'

PICTURE ACKNOWLEDGEMENTS

Front and back jacket – top **Hulton Getty Collection**
Front and back jacket – bottom **Chris Moore**
Advertising Archives /Revlon Consumer Product Corporation 120
Courtesy American Vogue 37, 128 right, /Duane Michals Copyright 1976 by the Conde Nast Publications Inc 124 left,/ Francesco Scavullo Copyright 1974 by the Conde Nast Publications Inc 128 right /Deborah Turberville Copyright 1975 by the Conde Nast Publications Inc 118 /119
Aquarius Picture Library 68 /69
Laura Ashley 121 left
Erwin Blumenfeld /Lisa Fonssagrives sur la Tour Eiffel 1939. Dress by Lucien Lelong. Photograph supplied by Kathleen Blumenfeld 58
Bridgeman Art Library /Alte Pinakothek, Munich 17, /Artemis, Luxembourg 20, /Biblioteca National, Turin 10 bottom, /Kunsthistorisches Museum, Vienna 14, /Musee du Louvre, Paris 11, 16 bottom, /Musee d'Orsay, Paris 21, /Palazzo Ducale, Mantua 10 top, /Palazzo Barberini, Rome 13, /Private Collection 15, /The Tate Gallery, London 18, 19, /Villa Farnesina, Rome 12, /The Victoria and Albert Museum 35
Copyright British Museum 8/9, 16/17
Copyright British Vogue, Conde Nast Publications 34, 45 centre, 61, 63 /Clive Arrowsmith 117, /Baron De Meyer 39 top, /Anton Bruehl 60, /Arthur Elgort 170, /Hoyningen-Heune 51 /Just Jaekin 101, 111, /Neil Kirk 143, /Sarah Moon 116 top, /John Rawlings 52 bottom, 66, 67, /Mike Reinhardt 119, /Jean Loup Sieff 96 left, /David Sims 162, /Steichen 55
Camera Press /Gene Fenn 86 top
Donald Christie /The Observer/Styling by Karl Plewka 174/175 main
Ossie Clark 102, 114/115, 128 left
Corbis-Bettmann 28, 70, 88, 92, 99 bottom, 103 right, /Reuter 155 top, /UPI 40, 46, 47 right, 49 bottom, 64 top, 74, 77, 79 top, 84 bottom, 86 bottom, 127 bottom, 129
Terence Donovan 110
Dover Publications 132 background, 137 background
Duffy 109
Mary Evans Picture Library 36
Hans Feurer /Nova 108
Copyright French Vogue /Bob Richardson 112 left
Geisler and Baumann /This photograph originally appeared in American Vogue 31 left
Andrea Giacobbe /The Face 1996 172
Ronald Grant Archive 89, 106, 122, 134 bottom
Hamiltons Photographers Limited /Horst P. Horst 57
Hulton Getty Picture Collection / 22 centre, 22 /23, 25, 33, 38 /39, 43, 44, 45 background, 49 Top, 52 /53, 65 top, 69, 71 bottom, 72 left, 72 /73, 75, 78, 79 bottom, 80, 81 top, 82 /83, 84 top, 85, 87, 90/91, 96/97, 98/99 top, 99 top right, 105, 113, 126, 130
Illustrated London News Picture Library 26
Nick Knight 146 (Courtesy of Yohji Yamamoto), 147
Marc Lebon /I-D Magazine 1986, 139
Peter Lindbergh /British Vogue 1990, 157
Copyright Man Ray Trust /ADAGP Paris,DACS London 1996, 56
Mander & Mitchenson 24
Mansell Collection 29 top, /Hoppe 41
Martin Margiela /Jennifer Levy-Lunt 165
Niall McInerney 127 top
Mirror Syndication International 47 left, 83, 104
Chris Moore 4/5, 100, 124/125, 125 bottom, 126 top, 132/133, 132 centre, 135 left, 136 top, 137, 138, 140, 141 top, 142, 144 left, 144/145, 145 top right, 150, 151 right, 152 bottom right, 152 top left, 154, 158/159, 160, 161, 164/165, 166 right, 167, 168, 169, 171, 173, 174

National Portrait Gallery /Paul Tanqueray 50
Queen /The National Magazine Co /Sandra Lousada 93
Harri Peccinotti 112 right
Private Eye /Kerber 148/149
Mary Quant 103 left
Rex Features 95, 97 bottom, 107, 116 bottom, 121 bottom, 134 top, 135 right, 136 bottom, 151 left, 152 top right, 153 bottom, 155 bottom, /Sipa-Press 115, 123
Selfridges Archives 64 /65
Courtesy of Sotheby's London /Cecil Beaton 48
Courtesy of Staley Wise Gallery /Louise Dahl-Wolfe 59
Sygma 145 bottom right, /Stephane Cardinale 149, /Julio Donoso 152 bottom left, /Keystone 30, 31 bottom, /Frederic de Lafosse 166 left, /Mark Mawson 153 top, /P. Vauthey 141 bottom.
Topham Picturepoint 27, 29 bottom, 32, 42, 71 top, 81 bottom
By Courtesy of the Board of Trustees of the Victoria & Albert Museum /Steichen 54
Vintage Magazine Co /Elle-Paris 94
With special thanks to the following for their help on this project:
David Hillman at Pentegram, Georgina Knight at British Vogue and Brian Baltin at American Vogue

Author's Acknowledgements: Special thanks to British Vogue for their time, effort and contribution from their unique archive.
To Lucinda Chambers fashion director of British Vogue, Joan Juliet Buck editor of French Vogue, Kate Moss and the staff at Storm, Ford Models, Jose Foncesca at Models 1, Peter Lumley, Caryn Franklin and i-D magazine, Caroline Baker, Nick Knight, Jeanloup Seiff, Terence Donovan and family of Erwin Blumenfeld and special thanks to Chris Moore and Maxine Millar for their time and assistance. For patience and support, a big thank you to family and friends, especially Vicki Reid.

Bibliography and further reading:
Ballard Bettina. 'In My Fashion.' *Secker and Warburg*, 1960.
Beaton, Cecil. 'Memoirs of the 40s.' *McGraw Hill*, 1972. 'The Parting Years.' *Weidenfeld*, 1954. 'The Wandering Years.' *Weidenfeld*, 1978.
Balmain, Pierre. ' My Years and Seasons.' *Cassell*, 1964.
Borel, Frances. 'The Seduction of Venus.' *Rizzoli*l, 1990.
Borzello, Frances. 'Notes From The Artists Model.' *Junction Books*, 1982.
Carter Ernestine. 'Magic Names of Fashion.' *Prentice Hall*, 1980.
Charles Roux, Edmonde. 'Chanel.' *Cape*, 1979
Chase, Edna Woolman. 'Always in Vogue.' *Gollancz*, 1954
Dawnay, Jean. 'Model Girl.' *Weidenfeld*, 1956.
Dahl-Wolfe, Louise. 'Photographers Scrapbook.' *Marker*, 1984.
Dior by Dior. *Weidenfeld*, 1957.
Gross, Michael. 'Model' *Transworld*, 1995.
Hall-Duncan,Nancy, 'History of Fashion Photography'
Harrison, Martin. 'Appearances' *Cape* 1991
David Hillman/Harri Peccinotti 'Nova' *Pavilion* 1993
Georgina Howell 'Vogue 75 Years'
Joie-Maie, Lepicard 'Givenchy 40 Years of Creation.' *Paris Musee* 1991.
Keenan, Bridget. 'The Women We Wanted to Look Like.' *MacMillan*, 1977.
Poiret, Paul. 'My First Fifty Years.' *Gollancz*, 1951.
Praline. 'Mannequin de Paris.' *Seuil*, 1951.
Seebohm, Caroline. 'The Man who was Vogue.' *Weidenfeld* 1982
Shrimpton, Jean. 'An Autobiography.' *W.H. Allen*, 1964.
Steichen, Edward. 'A Life in Photography.' *Garden City; Doubleday*, 1963.
Twiggy, 'Twiggy, An Autobiography.' *Hart-Davis, MacGibbon*, 1975.
Vreeland, Diana. 'D.V.' *Weidenfeld*, 1984.

360°